Black Children,
White Dreams

Black Children,
White Dreams

Thomas J. Cottle

With a Foreword by
Senator Walter F. Mondale

Houghton Mifflin Company, Boston

1974

First Printing v

Library of Congress Cataloging in Publication Data

Cottle, Thomas J
  Black children, white dreams.
  Bibliography: p.
  1. Negro children — Roxbury, Mass. 2. Children
and politics. I. Title.
F74.R9C67   301.45′19′6073074461   73-14534

Printed in the United States of America

For the Children

Woe unto them that decree unrighteous decrees, and that write grievousness which they have prescribed;

To turn aside the needy from judgment, and to take away the right from the poor of my people, that widows may be their prey, and that they may rob the fatherless!

ISAIAH 10:1–2

Acknowledgments

I WISH TO THANK FIRST the families of Roxbury who have given me nothing less than moments of their lives. Also, Leslie Dunbar and the Field Foundation, Marian Wright Edelman and the Children's Defense Fund of the Washington Research Project, the Education Research Center and the Medical Department of the Massachusetts Institute of Technology. In addition, let me thank Donald Cutler, William T. Donoho, Jr., Peter Edelman, Linda Glick, Cynthia Hooper, Merton J. Kahne, Karen Kane, Neil Kleinman, Betty-Marie Leising, Sara Lawrence and Orlando Lightfoot, Anita McClellan, Cynthia Merman, Sally Rogers, Judah Schwartz, Mady Shumofsky, Morrie Turner, Hugh Van Dusen, and Robert Wallace.

Gerald M. Platt and Eugene Lichtenstein must be singled out for their very special help and friendship.

Finally, Kay M. Cottle, my wife, has been involved more with this work, if that's possible, than with our prior work together. No doubt this is because of her abiding concern for the well-being of children and her insistence that they be protected and honored, and their voices heard.

Foreword

SEVERAL YEARS AGO an MIT professor named Thomas J. Cottle began visiting a number of families and children in the poor black section of Boston called Roxbury. But unlike many social scientists studying poverty in recent years, he did not count them, or counsel them, divide them into experimental and control groups, sample their opinions for a survey, or compare their lifestyles with those in other circumstances.

Indeed, much like Robert Coles, he listened . . . listened in particular to the thoughts, hopes, fears and dreams of two fifth graders—William D. Williams and Adrien Keller.

This deeply absorbing, poignant and personal book is the result. In it, these two black children express their beliefs and feelings about the 1972 election; politics in general; the meaning of laws; joblessness and underemployment; health care, crime and other issues. And through them we see these issues from a perspective few of us experience, and in human terms that escape the statistician or distant scholar.

When Adrien describes how her friend cries when he returns to see the public housing project still standing empty two years after his family and others were hurriedly evicted to permit demolition, the dislocations of urban renewal become more than interesting concepts.

That is the power of Tom Cottle's study. No one—least

of all the author—claims that the thoughts and feelings of William D. and Adrien accurately represent the thoughts and feelings of all, or even most, poor black children. And this book does not pretend to have the answers or solutions to any of the problems these children describe.

But in an age when there is decreasing communication between adults and children, and when our contacts with children outside our immediate families often consist of merely asking someone his age, or where she goes to school, this book reminds us how deeply thoughtful and sophisticated children are on a wide range of public issues.

At some point William D.'s mother gave Tom Cottle some very sound advice, and he took it. In discussing the goals of his visits, Mrs. Williams said:

> You get to know our family, we get to know you and your family. That they aren't equal, well, that's what we're all going to have to live with. Maybe together we'll change it. But right now I know it matters to William D., and Adrien Keller too, that you come. So keep coming. Only don't you try to teach them lots of things. Let them be teaching you. If that goes along with the kind of research you're doing, I can approve. Let them teach you, and let them, kind of, change you. That part of it may be even more important. There has to be change, and it only comes when someone's listening. So this time, you do the listening. Don't you go lecturing them.

Anyone else willing to take that advice will find this book to be a highly moving and enlightening experience. Because Tom Cottle listened so well, we can and should do the same.

Senator Walter F. Mondale, Chairman,
Subcommittee on Children and Youth

Introduction

IT HAS TO BE a very cold day for the streets named Wembley, St. Marks, Gloucester, South Plaine, Bowdoin, Temple, and McCall to be empty of children. Here, in the middle of the Roxbury district of Boston, a neighborhood of poor black families, the children seek out the streets for the space they provide, and for the adventures and friends that are to be found there. Some of the families in this neighborhood insist that whatever the weather, the streets are cooler in the summer, warmer in the winter, and just perfect for running and talking. Perfect, that is, if the children watch out for the traffic.

Once fashionable houses, the buildings in this neighborhood are of brownstone or brick and usually of four or five stories. Many have high arched window casings, patterned façades, and turrets, towers, and low latticed walls of cement on the roofs — all leftovers from an earlier architecture, a period of someone else's wealth. In the spring children leap about the roofs and towers, or jump from one roof to the next, but in the summer this play ends, for the tar becomes too hot for jumping or walking.

Inside the buildings are tile-floored entryways, mailboxes on the walls, and stairwells leading to the upper floors. All available space has been converted to apartments, typically with a living room, a small kitchen off it, and a couple of bedrooms. Most hallways, like large closets, were seen by landlords as wasted space, and so they were converted into smaller closets or tiny bedrooms able to accommodate a bed, dresser, and chair. Rarely will apartments have more than one bathroom. When they do, it is likely that the tenants use the second bathroom as a storage area or sleeping space for children, though the room is usually not remodeled. Toilet, sink, and bathtub, if there is one, remain.

Many families haven't enough chairs to seat all their members at a meal. Adults may sit on the floor, or more likely stand, while small children will sit on the laps of their brothers and sisters. And five or six children may sleep in a double bed.

For several years, I have been visiting with families in this Boston neighborhood at least once a week. I have met most of the families by chance, often through encounters with their children in the streets, at school, or after school in local restaurants, pharmacies, tailor shops, and flower stores, where in the winter it is particularly warm, and in pool halls too. We used to visit in the park on Wembley and South McCall, but the children no longer go there because the play equipment has rotted from the weather, the sandboxes have become pits in which animals defecate, and the ground is covered with scrap metal and garbage.

From the start, families learn that I might write about them, describing for others how their lives are led and how it is they are able to endure what they themselves call "life's most difficult hardships." In some cases, naturally, there is no friendship to be established; I am turned away by a family, and told not to speak with the children.

In the beginning, especially, my work generates problems for these families. Why have I chosen them? What really do I want of them? What kinds of things are they supposed to talk about with me? And how do we overcome the differences that showed in the instant of our first encounter, and the advantages I possess by nature of my position in society and my role in conducting the research?

Unlike many social scientists, I often have no good answers for these families. I use words like *description* and *observation,* and tell them I believe in having their words heard by those who live in other parts of America. The young children are not overly concerned with my stated purpose; they have already made their decision as to whether or not I look like a good bet for a friend. Older children and parents, for good reason, are more suspicious and scrutinizing, if not perplexed. In one regard, I am but another person coming to their home uninvited, ready to *take* something from them. On the other hand, they may feel that my presence, like that of any researcher, means a chance to talk and be heard, to be recognized; maybe, too, they are honored by this new friendship, however contrived it may seem at first. And so I do my best to convince them of my interest in them, and express my hope that they might be willing to share some hours with me. Sometimes, for as I say I am occasionally turned away, they will reply, in their way: I am not sure what this is all about, but I will take a chance, let you come in, and tell you what you want to know, or what you ought to want to know, and learn something of you and your children as well.

It is this cognitive hurdle, along with the political one, that makes these first encounters so uncomfortable. Besides the doubt, the natural belief that here is still another exploiting analyst or politician, and the obvious differences in our appearances and backgrounds, the absence of a specific problem or topic that might have brought me to them seems most unsettling. I constantly wish I could announce that it is their attitudes toward housing or schooling that I am after, but instead I turn again to the goal of describing their lives, listening to their words, and sharing experiences.

In the winter of 1972, the sort of clarification that many of the families sought from me was at last forthcoming. I finally heard one topic that seemed for the while to take precedence in my conversations with the children. The elections to be held later that year were provoking the children to tell more and more of their reactions to government and politics generally, and to reveal not only their knowledge and sophistication about these issues, but how deeply they felt the political realities of their neighborhood, their city and state, and America. No one should believe that the elections alone stimulated these children's search for knowledge about politics or created an air of special sophistication. Granted, not all children understand political complexities like the nature of compromise or the tensions caused by conflicting interests. But their political awareness of such issues as urban renewal, unemployment, housing, day care, education, health care, the mechanics of campaigns, food prices, and war predated any election that would be held in 1972.

"Don't say we don't know," children in this neighborhood remind me. "You remember those schools in the South that got integrated by little kids?"

"Yes," I respond, musing over their words, "do I remember?" Then they will use this historical moment as proof that young people understand the way government works. They tell me of the history of school desegregation, the dangers faced by families, the changes in the North and the South and in their own city, and look at me as if to say: Kids our age, younger even, did great things for America.

Along with clarifying a topic for the research, I selected two children whose lives I felt it especially important to follow through the months leading up to November. With their parents' permission, Adrien Keller and William D. Williams, eleven years old and fifth grade students in the Caldwell School which they walk to each day, agreed to share with me their knowledge of politics, and those parts of their private, interior world that they felt had been touched by the events, laws, bills, and programs the rest of us call, simply, daily political fare.

Throughout the year I maintained my friendships with the families of the neighborhood, but it was Adrien and William D., children who live eight blocks from one another, who became the center of my attention. My encounters with these two children and their families as the election drew close and finally arrived make up the story of this book.

I cannot say why, exactly, of all the children in the neighborhood, I specifically selected these two. As the work I will be describing is predicated on the establishment of care, as well as mutual acknowledgment and recognition, very human sorts of attractions play a role in the choice of friends and "subjects" for observation. Most of the children I know in the neighborhood could well have been chosen. Adrien and William D. do not seem to be any more intelligent, articulate, sophisticated, or even more politically concerned than these others. They did, however, appear a bit more relaxed with me, a bit freer, perhaps, to share opinions on political issues and the personal experiences that grew out of these issues. Perhaps, too, I felt more at ease in their presence, and better able to confront my own reactions to them, as well as the thoughts their words had evoked in me. Outside an early decision to include one boy and one girl, no formal criteria of selection were employed. It just evolved, really, that the boy would be William D. Williams, and the girl Adrien Keller.

As the reader will see, I make no pretense at objective assessments of people's lives, the inquiry being subjective and wholly dependent on my relationship with these families. The work rests on friendship and on paying attention to what is transpiring. One encounters people, listens to them speak about what matters to them, hears the attitudes and opinions they only naturally cultivate, and then records what they say. A danger, some might argue, is that Adrien and William D. are not representative of the urban poor black child. Moreover, as they are special in some way, if only because they meet with me, their words cannot be made the basis of generalizations about children's political views and sensitivities.

Actually, Adrien and William D. are careful to speak only for themselves. Even when I encourage them to characterize the political attitudes of their friends, they pull back slightly. Their parents, not surprisingly, are much the same way. Often I hear them suppressing an urge to begin a sentence with the phrase "Black people everywhere are . . ." Instead, they speak of their own lives and histories, and about what makes it possible for them to sustain themselves, their pride and dignity, in the face of all sorts of injustices. Thus, it is I who prefers to think that these families speak for a far larger group of people.

Still, the question of the representativeness of the two children in this book can be addressed, for children's political perceptions and knowledge have been studied. Indeed, the social and political features of urban poverty, especially of poor black families, and the cognitive, political, and social psychological development of these families have been the subject of literally hundreds of studies and accounts, only a small sample of which appears in the references of this book. Research performed with objective instrumentation on carefully chosen samples of American children reveal again and

again the political insights, sophistication, and concern dem-
onstrated by Adrien Keller and William D. Williams. The
work of Robert Hess, David Easton, Fred I. Greenstein, and
recently of Howard Tolley, Jr., Anthony Orum, and Roberta S. Cohen, among others, confirms the notion that children as young as eight and nine are being politically social-
ized to the extent that a measured hopefulness, sense of
efficacy, or an overriding cynicism becomes part of their personalities.

The story of Adrien Keller and William D. Williams does
not fall in the tradition of this objective form of inquiry. It
depends, as I have noted, on involvements with families over
long periods of time rather than on systematic measurements
of particular attitudes or degrees of knowledge. The intent,
moreover, is to describe sensitivities to political issues and
the ways these issues touch the lives of children and their
families in the course of living one day at a time. The work
is, therefore, closer to a tradition established by novelists,
cultural anthropologists, and journalists, among others, and
yet it is always complemented and enlightened by the more
traditional research of the social sciences.

Two final points remain to be made. First, I have
changed all names so that confidentiality may be preserved.
All those whose words appear in this book have read the
manuscript, or pertinent portions of it, and have granted
permission for its publication. Their reading provides a
check on the accuracy of reporting as well as a chance to
"hear" some conversations for the first time. In a few instances, actually, passages were deleted as the families felt
they might be harmful to the children.

Second, it must be understood that the families who have
consented to participate in this inquiry are not patients.
Although my method outwardly resembles the home visits

of social workers, none of these families has come to me re-
questing help or psychotherapy; and none of the families
has been selected because of some psychological problem any
was experiencing. Indeed, it is *I* who requested the right to
meet with *them*.

I hope, then, that the story of these two children will
again tell them and their families of my feelings for them
and my desire that our friendships endure. Even more, I
hope that in some way it will make a difference.

Black Children,
White Dreams

Chapter 1

IT HAS ALWAYS seemed to me that twelve-year-old
William D. Williams lives in the precise geographical center
of Boston. He doesn't, of course, but my trips to his home
in the Roxbury district not far from the Dorchester line
make me believe that I am about to enter the center of the
city. Most likely the importance to me of this one boy causes
this geographical distortion, but there is something, too,
about the congestion and density in his neighborhood. The
movement of people seems quick and abrupt, the passage of
time delineated and staccato. Then, too, there is my sense of
confinement in William D.'s neighborhood, the knowledge
that children play about these few streets, attend a nearby
school, but rarely travel even short distances to the downtown districts or the rural areas surrounding Boston. His
home is the center, then, because movement is confined and
a sense of expansiveness, space, and freedom is not to be felt
here.

I had known William D.'s mother for almost a year before
meeting him. We had worked together on a parent-teacher's
council at the local school, but I had never visited the Williamses' home or met Mr. Williams — William D. Senior —
or any of the five Williams children. There was never an
occasion, moreover, when I did not feel the hurts and anger
of the Williams family in my relationship with Mrs. Rosalie
Counter Williams. Even after three years our friendship re-

mains brittle. It is filled with her bitterness toward white people, and with the frustrations of not having money and of never being certain about one's job. It is filled, too, with the day-by-day work of watching over a husband and children, of keeping a house, and of wanting to improve the appearance and conditions of that house, and perhaps of an entire neighborhood. And then there is the perpetual desire to gain revenge, and the experience of having every political move she makes thwarted.

During those early months, despite the tension in our friendship, or perhaps because of it, Mrs. Williams described for me her sons' fights with black men and white men, and the struggles her husband endures at work. She recounted, too, the evening her daughter was driven home and carried up the apartment-house stairs by two policemen after having been raped and having had her cheekbone broken. Her dissatisfactions with the neighborhood schools were always part of the brittleness of our relationship, too, but even more so was her rage at city and state officials, who, she said, sent her community nothing but promises and rhetoric.

"If I ever meet one of these government dudes," she told me, "I'd sit him down where you're sitting now and tell him. You can just bet I would too. He'd come into Rosalie's house and they'd never get him out. I wouldn't let him up 'til he made a pledge with blood that he was going to help us out. Now, you arrange for that, you sit that man down right there where you're sitting now, and I'll say you've done something for us."

Mrs. Williams' assessments of me were no doubt influenced by the political realities she described and lived by. But there was a confusion as well about my role, an ambiguity that probably has never been wholly resolved. From the beginning she understood and accepted the researcher-writer part of my involvement with her family; but there was, in addition, the MI.T. professor-psychotherapist part, not to mention the differences of race and of what she calls "social standing."

"Tom's a doctor in learning," she told William D. in advance of my first visit with him. "If you can't learn about things from him, what with all his university credentials, then you can't learn nothing from anyone."

"Not even my teachers?" William D. questioned her, looking baffled.

"Nobody better," she answered him firmly, holding back her doubts about my role.

"*We* have certain things to teach him," she announced to me one afternoon, "and this school here has other things to teach him. But putting it all together, that's something *you,* with your position and all, ought to be able to do better than any of us around here. *You're* the professor. Now, don't you worry about this thing you call a perspective. You don't have to teach black children, mine or anybody else's, laws, or equal rights, or how they're different from anybody else. No one teaches that to *us.* We just want William D. to know what you have to say. We'll know by what he tells us what you two have been talking about. The left hand watches what the right hand's doing, and where the right hand's going. So, we'll keep an eye on William D."

Because of the ambiguity of my role, the tension with his mother, her way of always keeping me at arm's length, and my concern that he would not want to befriend me, my first meeting with William D. seemed especially important. It was a December afternoon and he had just returned from school. He was nine years old. When I entered the Williamses' home that day William D. was sitting in a chair in the living room perfectly still, his eyes firmly fixed on me.

One hand casually held a can of grape soda, while the other rested on his knee. But no matter where I moved his eyes never left me.

I looked at him from time to time as I spoke with his mother. His hair, I could see, was long and full, and a furrow made by his hat showed on the top of his head. It made him look as if he were wearing a crown. There were soft grooves under his eyes, and thin lines running within them. Although silent, he was a blaze of color in the room. His pants were bright red corduroy and they were topped by a green winter jacket rimmed with speckled gray fur. His gray boots had the appearance of suede and were tied with brilliant red laces. On one wrist he wore a watch held by a broad white leather band; on the other was a bracelet of clothesline rope with knots in it, a piece of jewelry he had made himself.

Being silent, I would learn, is not uncommon for William D. Even after two years, with our friendship continuing to grow, he may sit without speaking for long periods of time. Usually these periods occur when he is watching people, wholly engrossed in their actions, conversations, or manner. But they occur as well when no one is around, and he is lost in thought. As we became closer, I learned that William D. can be verbose, humorous, even comic; and that he has many smiles, my favorite of which is the one he exhibits when I show that I have understood a private reference that has passed between him and a friend.

His face is especially mobile and changing. At times, it resembles that of a child considerably younger than himself. He becomes alert, joyous, and his smiles are radiant. At other times, when he feels sad or angry, he appears older than eleven, and tired, as if he were aging more quickly than he was supposed to. I can never foresee, of course, just what mood I will discover on one of my visits, nor what direction our conversations will take. All I am certain of is that he will be at his home, sitting on the front steps — weather permitting — at the precise time we have agreed to meet.

His mother and father know this too. They have watched closely the way our friendship has evolved, and heard from William D. of the sorts of things we talk about. In one respect our intimacy has lessened Mrs. Williams' fears about my influence on William D. In another respect, however, her earliest doubts remain and always they are placed in a context of politics. "William D.," she told me once, after I had been visiting her son for more than a year, "waits for you as if he expected you to bring him messages from the White House itself." She smiled at her words and shook her head sadly. "Children" — she smiled again, looking far younger than her thirty-seven years — "are a lot like white folks. Thinking everything's just fine, most of the time. They'll change, though. You can be sure of that. At least the children will."

In the beginning, when Mrs. Williams gave her consent to my visiting with William D., she feared that I would fill his head with the same hypocrisies mouthed by powerful white people in the government. To counteract this possibility, she made certain that her own views were understood by all her children, and that I knew it was with uneasiness that she allowed William D. and me to meet.

Her consent still rests on a hope for change, and the chance, as she says, "that maybe someone somewhere might like to hear about *our* lives just for once." But there was a warning too that she communicated, as well as a guarantee that she sought: "It won't be too long now before William D. understands the way that whole political thing out there works. You're going to see it happen. One day you're going to ride up in that fancy red car of yours and little William D.'s going to come over alongside the driver seat and say: 'Okay, boss, the party's over. Black folks taking over now. Black folks sitting in the country's big cars now. Black folks turning the power into their hands.' You'll hear a man's voice coming out of him then. No more little boy. That'll be a man talking those words. I can see it. You getting out of that car and William D. sitting there giving you this long look, then pulling away from the curb. Varoom, all the smoke piling out of your tail pipe and my son riding off in your car." She stopped.

I heard an elevated train outside, dogs barking, a child yelling, "Give it to me or I'll break your head in," and a man calling out to the child, "Watch your tongue, Willis, or I'll come down there myself in a minute with a belt!" But Mrs. Williams seemed to hear none of it. She furled her brows as her fingers played with the shade of a lamp. Then she called off the reverie and looked at me: "You ain't scared by my words, are you?"

"A little, I guess." I thought of William D. with all that power, and of his someday being my adversary. I felt her impulse was to say: Good. Maybe she was thinking too, as she studied my face and saw my eyes turn away: Then be scared, so you'll know one shred of the feelings we all have living here like we do, underneath a government that couldn't care less about us except in November when two of *your* kind run for President. You're not merely part of the government, you *are* the government. The whole lot of them are rolled up in one hunk and you're it! *You're* what they send me.

"Don't be scared by what I say," she said at last. "I'm only doing some of my thinking out loud. You got something awful nice going with little William D., and I'm not about to call any halt to it. You two talk politics in the day and he talks politics with his father and me at night. So maybe in this way, all of us together can get him to become a United States senator someday. What do you think of that?" She laughed out loud and I wasn't sure whether or not to laugh with her. "Go on, laugh," she said. "That's a joke, bitterness and all. That's humor, seeing William D. as a senator. Maybe Mr. Brooke's successor. That's got to be one of the funniest jokes of the year." Angry sarcasm had replaced the humor. I didn't smile. She was adjusting the collar of her dress and pushing her hair away from the back of her neck and shoulders. "You got to have one helluva lot of white blood in you to become a black senator," she was saying. "One *hell*uva lot of white blood. Someday, maybe, instead of just talking with William D. down there" — she pointed toward the windows and the street three stories below — "you could pour some of your white man's blood into his. I'm beginning to think that might be more important than running around these streets trying to get people to go to the polls."

All of us maintain conceptions about poor black children. In part, the conceptions shape these children. We may believe that certain topics, like "children and the law" or "children and politics," mean little to them. We wouldn't expect, we say, a child "of that age" and "from that background" to know much about politics. And quite often children don't know about an issue. But sometimes we are astonished by what they do know, and how sophisticated their knowledge is about certain issues and conditions.

On a clear September afternoon three weeks before the elections, William D. and I were speaking about politicians and politics, and the kinds of things he talked about with his

friends. We had just come from looking in on a local precinct office where William D. liked to watch the people
working, and where he hoped that someday a famous politician would visit.

"Lot of kids here," he said, "know a whole lot of things
about politics. Elections come and everybody studies up on
them. We hear people talking, and we got lots of folks coming to our house asking us all sorts of questions."

"Questions like what?"

"Well, like whether we're going to vote. I can't vote, you
know . . ." he said with a certain serious formality.

"I know . . ." I said seriously.

". . . but I listen to what my folks say. Everyone around
here knows something about politics. Big-time politics, like,
they'll say. But around here you have to learn a lot about
politics just to, like, stay alive. Folks like me have to learn
all about welfare and why people go on it and off it. Got to
learn about taxes too. In Boston, folks pay a lot of money
when it comes to taxes. Breaks these families, especially the
men. Don't think it doesn't. Breaks 'em right in two. Tax
bill comes right out of their check, it's just like some big
dude going, FOOM, right into 'em." He suddenly stopped
walking and slammed his knee into the groin of an invisible
person in front of him. His face showed tightness and defi-
ance. Then slowly he lowered his leg. "It kills these men.
Women too. Kills the children too 'cause they know about
it. Sometimes we even talk about it in school. But they got
it wrong about what they say. Like, you hear, unemployment isn't the only thing bad. It's when a man works just as
hard as he can and even after that he doesn't have near
enough money to live by."

"Men you know, William D.?" I asked.

"Lots of 'em." He seemed sad. Several thoughts seemed to
fill his mind. I wondered whether one of them had to do

with his father working hard and still not earning the money
he requires.

William D. was looking down and not saying anything. I
imagined him twenty-five, thirty years from now chatting
with a group of his friends. His father by that time would
be a man in his sixties. William D. would be telling them:
My father's worked his ass off every damn day of his life
from the time he was six. Working, scuffling, scraping together anything he could lay his hands on just so the rest of
us could eat. But he's never complained. Did what he had
to do and kept his mouth shut. He worked just as hard as
any man who ever walked on this earth, and all he got for it
was about two bucks an hour from which he got to keep a
buck sixty maybe. If he was lucky. Now, if you all want to
get involved with politics, then you change the law that says
a man can work that hard and get so little. The men listening to William D. would nod agreement, for their fathers
had experienced the same thing. And something else would
tie them together — this fact of underemployment was
known to them when they were nine and ten and eleven.

"What're you thinking, William D.?"

"I don't really know. Different things. See all those folks
working in that place?" he asked, possibly turning the conversation back to precinct offices and politics in my behalf.
"I'd sure like to get a job working in there with them someday."

"You can get a job in there," I assured him.

"Not the kind I want, though." He was smiling, but his
eyes remained fixed on the sidewalk. "I want to be the candidate, man. That's the job in there I really want. Hell,
most of those cats are just going to go around ringing door-
bells day of the voting so everybody will go and vote. They
make all sorts of promises to 'em."

"Like what?"

"Well, like this year they've been promising people that if they vote for old 'Govern they'll give 'em a little Christmas tree." He shrugged his shoulders. "Ain't no Christmas tree going to help folks around here, though. Seems to me that that's sort of the wrong thing to do."

"Are Nixon people doing the same thing?"

"Hell no, man. You don't even see those people around here. They know folks around here have nothing to do with that guy. He wouldn't ever come around here. I'm pretty sure of that."

"Did McGovern?"

"No. He didn't come either. Hey" — he suddenly shifted — "you know what really gets me is the way these politicians go running around kissing all those children." He was shaking his head. "I think that stuff sucks. They really don't have any plans to do anything for 'em so why they think they have to go through all those motions like you see every night on television? If they ever came around here I'd talk straight to 'em. I wouldn't let 'em shake my hand until I heard what they had to say."

The parents of this neighborhood are not surprised by the political knowledge and sensitivity of their children. Neither are the older brothers and sisters, ministers and teachers. These people know, if only because they live with the children and talk to them. They attend to the children, and they pay attention. They ride on buses with children, walk with them and go to ball games with them, and put them to sleep at night. By the time children like William D. reach eleven, these people can almost see the layers of years that in miraculous fashion become the young personality and the personal outlook. At very least they can recall a child's history and recount the significant moments of that child's growth.

William D.'s oldest brother, Archie, a serious young man of seventeen with a love for science and athletics, says that at times William D. acts like a two-year-old. "He gets all upset when things don't fall his way. He's a damn little crybaby." His older sister, Gloria, whose handsome appearance always makes her look much older than her sixteen years, persists in seeing the seven- or eight-year-old boy in William D. She becomes angry when William D. acts irresponsibly, claiming that at his age he should not have such foolish fantasies and daydreams.

William D. himself is quick to recognize what he calls the childishness in himself and other people. In August, for example, a group of his friends and I were standing on the sidewalk on Hanover Street talking about the campaign. Because the story had been on television day after day, it was not long before someone mentioned Senator Thomas Eagleton's name. "Hey, what *did* happen there?" ten-year-old Nate Thayer asked the rest of us.

"He quit!" Johnnie Nightengale answered. "He was going to be Vice President, see, but he quit. Got sick."

"Nah, that ain't the reason why," Nate argued. *"Is* that the reason? For true, Tom?"

William D. knew about the Eagleton matter but he was eager to hear my explanation. He ordered his friends to be quiet.

"I know only what the newspapers said," I began, "but it seemed that Senator Eagleton had been treated in a mental hospital in Saint Louis. Because of this, many people wondered whether he should still be the vice-presidential candidate. In the beginning Senator McGovern felt that Senator Eagleton was courageous to admit these problems openly and said that he should remain as the candidate. But after a while, people had serious doubts about him and so he resigned. But," I added, "it's often difficult to know exactly what is happening in situations like this, for the newspaper stories do not always say the same things, and certain facts cannot always be reported."

"That's always the way it is with politics," William D. announced when I finished speaking.

Johnnie Harrelston wanted a turn to speak but Nate beat him to it. "I know all about that mental thing like that Eagleton had," he was saying. "See, when I was a kid, I had it done to me."

"Yeah? You a mental or something, Thayer?" Barney Jacquet asked.

The others looked incredulous. "What'd you do?" they wanted to know. "Where'd it happen?"

"In the washer place, not too far from here." Nate Thayer went on to describe how an aunt punished him one afternoon by shutting him in a dryer for a few minutes. He remembered how hot it had been inside, and how his breath condensing on the glass window of the dryer made it impossible for him to see out. He was sure he was going to die.

"That's what Eagleton had, I mean, something like that, isn't it?" Nate asked me. The other boys seemed stunned. Nate's story had frightened them. Before I could repeat my definition of the term "electroshock treatment" and clarify some other details for them, William D. began to speak.

"That ain't what happened, Thayer. Man, are you ever dumb! Here's what it is. The guy worked hard, real hard doing all the things he did, and then he just went crazy for a little while. That's all it was. He had to go to the hospital, but lots of people go crazy just like he did, especially politicians."

"Why politicians?" Johnnie and Phil Hawkins wanted to know.

"Because," William D. started, "they work hard. That's one reason. The main reason, though, is that they lie so much, after a while they can't live the same way they've been living no more."

"You're crazy, man," Phil shouted at William D. "It's like Nate here was saying."

"Nate's right," Johnnie agreed. "It's punishment!"

William D. acquiesced. "Well, maybe that's it," he said. "Maybe that's it. But Nate's talking like a child. You're always acting like a child, Thayer."

"Hell I am." Nate did his best to defend himself.

"Politicians go crazy from all their work, don't they, Tom?" William D. looked to me for support. "Even the guys in the government. They're all going crazy. Maybe 'cause they're crooks or something too. It gets 'em down the kind of things they have to do, so they go crazy. It's just the way it is."

I had never seen William D. angry. It seemed as if he wanted to attack Nate Thayer.

"You're a little baby, Thayer," he kept yelling. "You don't know anything about politics, talking on here about being shut in a dryer. Shit, that's crazy. If I ever heard anything crazy in my life that's it."

Then, without warning, William D. grabbed the comic book Nate was holding, threw it to the ground, and stomped on it. "You ain't never going to learn anything about politics if you read shit like that. You better start reading the newspapers, man. You read those comic books you'll be a baby all your life. You're a baby is what you are. You're a fucking *baby!*" It was only then that the others intervened. For the first time I saw that William D. was crying.

The conversation among the five of them that followed was filled with anger and bitter accusations. They jabbed at each other about being crybabies, they talked about politics, their parents and teachers. Phil, Barney, and William D. even got going on comparing the intelligence, physical strength, and cunning of older brothers, a topic that made them even more tense. Soon they were pushing at one another, walking away down the street in disgust, screaming back over their shoulders, then returning again.

At last the group disbanded and William D. and I headed out together down Gloucester Street in the direction of his home. We walked along in silence, and it appeared that he would not tell me what was clearly troubling him. Then quite abruptly, he turned to me. "See, when I was a kid, my grandfather went nuts. They took him to a hospital, or someplace like that. I never saw him again, but I remember the day they came and took him away. I remember that real well. You should have seen him. He was really crazy. He really was. He was jumping around speaking all kinds of words in this weird language. I couldn't understand him. No one could understand him. My mother was trying to calm him down and stuff, but he'd get excited. Then, like all of a sudden, he'd just stop and wouldn't move at all. He'd just be standing there, you know, like he was a wall or a car or something. Not alive, I mean. Then after a while, he'd go all crazy again, like before, and scream at me.

"Just before the doctors came he ran away from my mother where she was holding him in the front hall of our house, and grabbed me by the arms. Jesus. I was only eight or nine, I guess, and he grabbed me and said I should help him. My mother, she was pulling him away and he was holding on to me. The lamp in the front hall fell over and crashed down and made this big noise. Boom! My mother was holding him and trying to grab it at the same time. She caught the shade but the lamp broke. Anyway, my grandfather was going on crying that I should help him 'cause they were going to take him to the hospital and kill him. Electrocute him."

William D.'s voice was excited, just as it had been when he took on Nate, Johnnie, and the others. "He kept saying I could help him. 'Don't let 'em 'lectrocute me,' he kept yelling. 'Don't let 'em 'lectrocute me.' I didn't know what to do. I kept looking at him and my mother. She was crying but you could tell she was really mad at him too. She kept saying, 'Shut up or I'll whip your face.' It was like he was one of the children. Later on that night I was crying. I asked Archie what my grandpa meant by 'lectrocution.' I thought maybe he'd been a criminal or something. Maybe killed somebody. Maybe he was going to die because he was crazy. I was real young then so I didn't know anything about mental hospitals. He said, 'No, he isn't going to die.' "

"But he *was* going to be given electroshock therapy?" I asked.

"Yeah, whatever it's called," William D. said softly, his fright receding.

"I think that's what they call it, William D."

"Then that's it."

For almost a block he said nothing. We just walked along down Gloucester and then turned onto Bowdoin Street. William D. was gazing down at the ground; I was studying his face. "Just like that dude who was supposed to be the Vice President got?" I heard him ask finally.

"Well, maybe something like that, I suppose."

"Guess he must have been really crazy then. I mean crazier than all the other politicians. I mean, ready for the loony bin. Like my grandpa."

"No, I don't think so," I explained. "He must have been exhausted and depressed. That's all. He's perfectly fine now."

"What's that mean?" he asked, peering up at me.

"Exhausted?"

"No, that means tired. The other word. Depressed."

"Very, very sad. Maybe a little angry too."

"Yeah," William D. mused. "I guess my grandpa must have been sad too. He didn't ever have that much in his life. My grandmother died a long time ago, way before I was born, even. So there was nothing especially good about his just getting older and sicker like he was getting. I guess he must have been sad. I never thought about it that way. But Nate still didn't know what he was talking about. He *is* a baby, you know. You saw him."

"Is that what Archie called you that night they took your grandfather away to the hospital? A baby?"

"Yeah. It was. You're pretty smart, Tom. How'd you figure that out?"

Trying to keep him from feeling too unhappy, I told William D. that if he would smile for me just once before we reached his home I would tell him. He responded by giving me the widest and most disingenuous grin I had ever seen. It was so outrageously fake that I began to laugh. My laughter made him laugh.

"A little birdie told me what was in your mind," I said.

"That's a lot of shit," he came back, hitting me on the arm and pushing me off stride. "Some bird. Some bird. I wonder, though, what fixed it so that these two men should end up having the same thing. You think of that, Tom? Now that's a real coincidence. Here you got two guys having the same thing go wrong with them. Both cracking up. Both, like you say, getting real sad and all that, and having to be electrified or whatever you call it . . ."

"Electroshock treatment." I repeated the words for him.

"Yeah, that thing. And here they are, one real rich and going to be the Vice President, and the other real poor, maybe not even going to vote for him. Fact is he can't vote now."

"Why's that?"

" 'Cause he's dead."

Chapter 2

WHILE WILLIAM D. was content to speak with me almost anywhere, his favorite meeting place was in a booth at the Maynard Restaurant on the corner of Maynard and Temple streets. His pattern was always to run inside the restaurant and make a dash for an empty booth, leaving me to order for him. Because so much about him caused me to regard him as older than he actually was, I was surprised when he did something childlike, dashing for a booth without thinking about who would order or pay.

One day we agreed to meet at the restaurant, and when I arrived William D. was already sitting in a booth by the window. He had seen me come in and watched as I waited at the counter for our food. Soon he was looking around at the people, and, in his way, examining them. Everyone in the restaurant was black, with the exception of myself and one older man working in the kitchen as a dishwasher.

The simple scene of the restaurant reminded me that something in the environment can always bring me closer to William D., and then just as easily push me away from him again. Here I was, a white man in his mid thirties from a prestigious university, dressed in slacks and a sports jacket, accompanying an eleven-year-old black boy to a restaurant in the middle of a black neighborhood, his neighborhood. Indeed, it is precisely the kind of uneasiness I felt in that restaurant that dissuaded me from visiting with William D.

at the university or in other neighborhoods where he would feel foreign and uncomfortable. However, it was not only the sense of uneasiness that I felt but also the absurdity of the situation. As important as our friendship and the research were to me, the idea that this boy, now looking about the restaurant, was waiting to discuss with me his views on school busing — for we had agreed that this would be one of our topics of the day — seemed almost foolish. Quite likely, these were the same feelings of absurdity that Mrs. Williams had revealed to me when we first talked of my interest in meeting William D. I remembered suddenly how she looked me over, trying to envision, perhaps, her son walking about the streets of Roxbury with me at his side.

No doubt I feel more comfortable with William D. when we are alone, and particularly in his home. Whatever tensions are caused by the differences between us are lessened by the feelings of home and family. It is as if nothing can happen there, whereas here in the restaurant I feel that someone might take exception to our friendship or to my role as observer and recorder. Then too, there is something about being one of two white men in a restaurant frequented mainly by black people.

William D. watched me lay out hamburgers, French fries, and milkshakes on the table. My actions could not have appeared more casual.

"You scared in here?" William D. asked when I was finished.

"Why'd you ask that?"

"You're the only white dude in the place I can see, you know."

"I know. So?"

"Just asking."

"You want catsup?" I asked.

"Yeah. You got some?"

"Do I ever forget anything?"

"Don't know. I'll know when I see what you write."

"You're making me nervous," I told him, starting to smile. His mouth was already filled with food. Then, as he was about to speak, William D. recognized someone outside in the street. It was Marvene Travis, a friend of his from school whom I had met. She was glad to see both of us, but I hoped she would not interrupt us just now. So often, when William D. and I were in the middle of wonderful conversations, other children sought to join us. Within a few minutes they had distracted him, taken him away from me. Those were the times I would see him as a child and find myself thinking of him as thoughtless, unfriendly, even disrespectful. In truth, he was none of these, but young people running together often seem less tender and vulnerable — tougher and invincible. And they don't let us in.

"Come on inside." William D. signaled her frantically.

"I can't," she mouthed through the glass, then waved to me, mimicked William D. eating by blowing out her cheeks, and continued to laugh at us. She was rubbing her stomach to tell us of her hunger, then she turned, blew us a kiss, and raced for a bus.

I waved but she didn't see me. William D. smeared a French fry against the glass then looked around sheepishly to see if he had been observed. I handed him a napkin and reminded him of our "formal topic" for the afternoon, busing.

"Oh yeah," he said, still with a mouthful. The sound of his words garbled by the food only made him laugh. He looked one last time for Marvene but she had disappeared.

"Busing," he said at last. "Me and busing. And politics. Can't forget that," he added, assuring me he had not forgotten my research. "Busing is what you really want to talk about, isn't it?"

"Not unless you want to talk about it. Though I think it's awfully important right now." He could tell that I wanted to hear about it.

"Busing, you see," William D. began, "is just another word for integration. See, most folks are very happy to have us niggers living where we live." Behind William D. I saw a man turn around slowly to stare at him. His eyes were glassy and his eyelids were heavy. He had been startled by William D.'s words. As if he had been unfairly awakened he turned back to his coffee and let his head fall forward again. "Then, when they feel up to it, they go around and say, 'You and you and you' " — William D. was pointing to invisible children — " 'get up and go out there to the suburbs and wake those folks up. Don't get 'em out of bed or nothing, you know, not too much trouble, just wake 'em up.' So we're the ones they pick."

Without inflection in my voice, I said that it sounded as though he disapproved of busing.

"No, that ain't right at all." He was stuffing more potatoes into his mouth. "That ain't what I mean. What I mean is that the President and all those big cats, they can't come right out and say they don't like black folks. That ain't the way. So they turn the whole thing around, make believe they love all the children in the world, no matter what color they are, and keep pushing this neighborhood-school jive on us. It's a lie. Everybody *knows* it's a lie. They're just trying to keep communities from being integrated." He stopped, almost surprised by where he had arrived. "And I guess I don't know what I think of that.

"Busing, see, is one of the ways the big cats get the little cats to dance around. Move 'em here, move 'em there. Or maybe I should say the government doesn't like busing 'cause rich folks don't want to be upset. I'm not upset that I'm not being bused anywhere. But if you've ever talked to those folks in the suburbs, whew, they can really go crazy when you tell 'em that black folks are coming."

"You've talked to them?" I asked.

"Well, not really." The eagerness and verve were suddenly gone from his voice and he sounded embarrassed. "But you know what I'm talking about. White folks, like you see on the television, man, they get all steamed up when someone says they're going to bring some black children into their schools. You wouldn't think that anything could get them to be so upset. I mean, I know lots of black children, and I don't think they're so bad. Not in any way that I could see."

William D. went on to tell me stories he had heard about families wanting their children to be bused to suburban schools as well as families who were angry that the neighborhood schools were not good enough. He remembered two women arguing in the kitchen of his home. One wanted her children to be bused to a grammar school that happened to be fifteen miles away. She insisted that busing was the only chance for her children, but the other woman argued that she wanted to have all her children in schools close by where she could reach them quickly if they ever needed her. His own mother hadn't said a word, and William D. never asked what she thought. His father, however, on another occasion, told him that "busing was a good thing, but that maybe, in a few years, it wouldn't be necessary if the local schools were improved. The schools in the neighborhood could be so fine," his father had said, "that white children in the suburbs would want to come to them. But it isn't the case now."

Overhearing us in the restaurant, some people might have believed that William D. does not want to be bused, or perhaps that he is envious of those students who are bused. I know that he meant something else. His attitudes toward busing are made up of the hurts experienced by all the members of his family. He carries the knowledge that what is called "equal opportunity" has never showed its face in the Williams household; that both his parents are unable to find jobs that coincide with their gifts and schooling; and that his own future is much in question even though his talents and capacities are obvious. At eleven, he is already burdened by the weight of politics, not of ideology or debatable theory, but of the law, regulation, and open dispute. I must constantly remind myself that at times politics for him is encompassed in the angry warning his mother once gave him in my presence: "Don't cross the street into another neighborhood or you'll get whupped. Someone will be there to whup you, so don't you go that way. Don't you ever go that way again."

What William D. means, therefore, when he says that busing complicates his life is that there may be good and proper reasons why black people live with the conditions they do. How, after all, can he defend the shabbiness of this restaurant to the one white person he can see? Perhaps these are the conditions that are meant to be. For while his childlike eyes see the painful disparities and inequalities all about him, his adultlike visions of society and politics make it impossible for him to see how conditions and circumstances might be made different. For the moment, in the restaurant, I represent to him the fundamental political disparity. With all his strength, sensitivity, and assuredness here in all-black surroundings, he is nonetheless constrained by my age, status, and color. As open as he is about some matters, the natural diffidence of childhood coupled with the bitter diffidence of racism silences him.

Much of the politics that some of us think is prac-

ticed over the heads and thereby out of the reach of children affects them more deeply than we might realize. The
debates over busing have taught William D. that everything
about his life, his place in American society, is questionable.
They have taught him that people doubt him, and therefore, he is forced to believe, his talents, his family, his parents' occupations, his religion, and his ancestors too. This
fact is drummed into *my* head by what he says, almost says,
or is afraid and unable to say: "I doubt me." And it turns
out, when one examines the history of his family, that his
reasoning has not been exagerated.

"I think they should bus the white kids here," William D.
was saying. "Lots of folks around here don't feel good about
the way they're living and working, so maybe that's why no
one talks about it. But we learn lots of things too, you
know. Isn't everything that's good going on in those rich
places." As he spoke, another idea came to him. "Whoever
gets elected, he should mix up all the neighborhoods."
William D. seemed elated, and holding on to a hamburger
and French fries, his hands froze in space. "That's it. Nixon
or 'Govern, if he gets elected, I mean, they could make this
rule for the people that they're going to mix up all the communities. Send people helter-skelter all over the place.
Nobody knows where they're going to end up. Some go
here, some go there. Maybe they'll have to send out orders.
Like, Thomas Cottle — you got a middle name, Tom?"

"Yes. Joseph. J.," I replied, surprised by his question.

"Yeah. J.," he mused. "Thomas Joseph Cottle, you got
your orders here to live in . . . in . . . Roxbury, Massachusetts." William D. began to laugh out loud and shake his
head. I heard him stamping his feet under the table.
" 'Roxbury, sir,' " he went on, mimicking me. " 'Why, sir,
there must be some mistake. I mean, I'm rich, I don't live

in places like *Rox*bury.' 'Well sir' " — now it was the voice of the imagined commanding officer — " 'these here are your orders, so you better pack your bags and get right down here at once 'cause we got some other folks moving into your house right this very minute.' " He checked his watch and made an expression of excessive self-importance. " 'Yessir, the exchange is on right now!' " Still shaking his head, he crammed more potatoes into his mouth. "Wow, that'd be the day, wouldn't it? If old 'Govern put that on his ticket he'd shake 'em up pretty good, wouldn't he?"

The idea both amused and frightened me. I had never heard William D. speak of private ownership or use the word "capitalism" as I have heard it used by children in other communities. Still, it was an enforced movement of the population he now was advocating, and how this movement was being played out in his imagination clearly delighted him. At the same time, I was feeling uncomfortable, partly because I knew there were things he was not about to share with me, and partly too because the house I own must in some complicated ordering of political fate be balanced by the tenement in which his family along with nine other families lives. It is the naive idea of the mathematics that some-one must come down if someone else is to rise that nagged at me. Is that true? I wondered, looking at his face. Is it true that the rich must come down if the poor are to ascend? Is it true that if children are to achieve, or just get along, then we, their elders, must forfeit some part of our space and re-sources? Is it true that parents *inevitably* sacrifice for their children? Or is this all merely the traditional guilt uttered by those who cannot openly admit to children that they feel they are owed in some way?

What *is* true is that at this moment William D. had made me think of losing my home, of being moved against my will and without recourse to a part of the city I cannot call my own. It is a fantasy, naturally, although it possesses a peculiar power because someone so young has initiated it. Even more, he has initiated it by combining whimsy with bitterness, and that makes the fantasy all the more frightening and the act of getting close to him all the more difficult. In these moments, I want very much to invoke my so-called clinical skills with him, if not hide behind them altogether.

The goal, I tell myself, turning away from personal feelings to safer conceptualizations, is to help, not colonialize. Yet colonialization and paternalism seem to be natural responses in some people when dealing with children. And despite many criticisms, children sometimes feel protected, even uplifted by these responses. Still, fatherly if not paternalistic responses are also made in reaction to personal threat and attack.

"Who would you vote for if you could, William D.?" I asked him, putting these other thoughts out of my mind.

"You mean between 'Govern and Nixon?" he asked from across the table in our special booth.

"Yeah. Who would you vote for?"

"Let me think."

"Take your time."

"They give you time in those voting places to make up your mind?" he wondered.

"Well, some time, but I think they think you're supposed to know who you're going to vote for when you go in. But you can have some last-minute considerations."

"Okay, I'm thinking." He waited. "Child contemplating politics" was the caption I saw beneath an imagined photograph of William D. in that restaurant. Or, "Child eating politics." He looked terribly serious, studious actually. I wanted to reach out and touch him, but I didn't.

Politicians contemplate similar things. They go out into

the world and touch people, the voters, their constituencies, their children, shake their hands and look them in the eye. They wade into those airport and Main Street crowds touching everyone in sight. Then the people go home touching over and over again the places where they have been touched. Shake the hand that shook the hand that shook the hand . . . Or maybe by touching one creates the ambience, the environment, a certain state of being. Perhaps there is no genuine feeling of life, or feeling *for* life, until one has touched others and allowed them in this way to feel the tingling of their own nervous systems. Strange, that in having this thought I should feel sad sitting in a half-filled restaurant talking politics to William D. From nowhere, sadness overtakes me. I reason that it emerges spontantaneously in the situation of the two of us together, but it does not disappear. No matter who is elected on the first Tuesday of November or the Tuesday four years later, my sadness will be there.

The sadness is explained somewhat by another thought. Politics, I theorize silently in William D.'s presence, is an enterprise of fathers. They touch, often only to be touched, not always to support and give. Thus far, women in politics are almost immediately turned into fathers; busy, away, needing what they need when they need it, but not having the time to remain in constant contact. But a mother touches, knowing that the contact is needed by the child. How, then, does one get politicians to feel this way, to realize that, in a sense, the touch, and the sense of care it implies, is the ultimate act.

Perhaps my sadness is connected to a sense of impending loss or separation from someone. From William D., maybe.

"What are you touching me for? What do you want?" It was William D.

"I'm just thinking you're a good man."

"Back off, man. Here, okay, shake my hand."

We shook hands.

"So, William D., who you voting for? That's why I touched you," I stumbled.

"Why's that?" He appeared confused.

"I thought you were falling asleep in the voting booth there and we got a line of people waiting to vote."

"Shoot." He said the word slowly. "You kidding me?"

"Yeah, I am."

"Shoot." It was said even more slowly this time. He paused for a moment looking at me, through me perhaps. "I ain't voting for no one. No one here I'd vote for."

"Why not?"

"Nobody out there running who speaks for me. President has to represent you, right?"

"Supposedly."

"Well, neither 'Govern or Nixon can do that for me. No way they can do it. They ain't black, neither of 'em, and they don't have no black friends with 'em. Whenever you see 'em they're always with white people. They ain't even got women with them, except their wives once in a while, but that don't mean anything. That's just to make sure that everybody knows they're married and have a family and stuff like that. If Nixon really wanted to do something he'd make sure we all had money. Not the people who don't work, I mean the people who work all the time or want to work. Like me. I want to work but I can't find jobs around here. And around here is the only place that the city lets me look. Kids that are bused out, you know, like we were talking before, they got other places they can go looking for jobs. That's what they tell me, anyway. But around here, they got old men doing some of the jobs I could do. I'm old enough, but I can't fight it. Those guys need the money more than I do. So if they really wanted to do a good thing as President, then they'd give us jobs. Give me jobs, anyway. Give my mother a better job than being a dishwasher, and make it so's my father would earn more money where he works. He ought to earn as much as you earn. My brother should too."

"Which means that you should earn this amount too then, someday," I offered respectfully.

"Me? I get to earn more." He grinned. "I'm going to need more anyway. Old Nixon, he's going to raise those taxes so high ain't no one around here going to be able to pay for anything anymore. You see if he doesn't. I'm going to be twelve in, let's see now, three months. Okay? Now, can you imagine all the money I'll have to pay the government when I get to be twenty-two, then thirty-two? They just keep raising the taxes and only the rich cats have the money. And they get off not paying their taxes the way they do. So, since the whole thing's not fair anyway, I can't see any reason why I should vote, I mean, if I could vote and all. Shit, man, the way I look at it, he only let the young people vote 'cause he wants more taxes from 'em."

"I don't follow that, William D. The right of eighteen-year-olds to vote is not supposed to be connected to what they're earning or what they're paying in taxes."

"They don't?" William D. was revving up his argument. "Well, they may not now," he retreated momentarily, "but you wait and see what happens. If he gave 'em the vote, he's figured out some way to get the bread from 'em later on. You'll see if he don't." Suddenly an idea struck him and pulling back in the booth he accidentally kicked me. "I'm sorry, man." He laughed.

"Jesus, I'm getting it from all sides."

"I'm really sorry, man, I didn't mean it."

"I'm teasing. Don't worry," I assured him.

"But what I was thinking was that it seems to me that the richer you are, the better it is to vote. 'Cause even if you vote when you're poor nothing helps you. What I was thinking was that all these young people" — he looked at me — "I mean some of these young people, are going to be surprised when they find out that they can vote but that voting isn't going to help 'em."

"The poor ones, you mean?" It was an unnecessary question.

"Of course I mean the poor ones," he replied. "It's always the poor ones, ain't it? It's always the poor ones that I see, anyway, believing something's going to come to them. Then they're real surprised and disappointed. Sometimes, you know, poor folks are worse than children. They get it in their heads that things are really going to go great for them. Like they were promised a Christmas present or something. I'll see 'em standing around, you know, dreaming about all the good things going to happen. Then somebody will say, 'Ain't nothing coming here. Poor folks going to get nothing again this year. Just like last year, you know, so stop dreaming.' Then they go off mumbling somewhere. I don't know how to explain it. You've seen 'em that way so you know what I am talking about." He continued quickly so as not to let me interrupt. "But like I was saying, they're children. Whining and all. They ain't never going to get anything by whining. Course they haven't got too much by all the voting they've done either. I talked to this man, you know? He said this is going to be his sixteenth time voting." William D. was shaking his head. "How old does that make him anyway?"

"Well, he probably means that he's voted for President sixteen times, so, I guess, it puts him in his eighties maybe."

"Man, he's seen a lot of Presidents, ain't he? And what do they bring him, I'd like to know? He still lives in a run-down little place. Kids I know used to go there and mess around in all this junk he's got in his back yard there. Sixteen times in the voters' booth is a whole lot of waiting." William D. became silent. He was peering out the window at the street but not focusing on any one sight. His face showed strain, a thoughtful intensity that for some reason made me try to imagine how he would look forty or fifty years from now. I suspect that William D. himself might have been dreaming of being old enough to have voted six-teen times, but I didn't ask him to tell me his thoughts. "No sir," he went on, "the young are going to see their vote won't matter much. At least the poor young folks. And anyway it's all fixed."

"What is?"

"The election."

"It is?" Why had I sounded so incredulous, when during my own childhood I heard hundreds of stories of campaign fraud and vote manipulation? They even had dead people voting when I grew up.

"Sure, man, you don't know that?" William D. was play-ing the role of surprised political-science professor. Where have you been, young man? was brimming over in his tone. "Sure, this voting thing is all a pile of shit. You go through all the motions like you're really voting, right?"

"Yeah?" He was making me feel I had been betrayed by my own government; as if fraudulent vote-counting was com-mon practice that everyone knew about.

"Okay, then they take all the votes and mess a little here and then add a little there. Then they come out with a final number. Then they add up all the sections of the city, or whatever they do, and if the vote isn't the way they want it they change it and turn all the numbers in to the newspapers and the television. Then they report it. Maybe it's right, maybe it ain't. No one knows and no one cares. You're going to go home and tell the old lady that you voted, right, so what do you care?"

"So why do people vote then?" No doubt I can match William D. in listing the corrupt and evil features of our society. Probably, too, I can impress him and his family with my dreams and plans for a new society and the changes that must be made quickly if people like the Williamses are to live in genuine freedom. Yet despite all this, I realize that a part of me still holds to the idea that people vote for their leaders and that their vote is counted and matters. Perhaps that is naive; perhaps that is why I appear defensive in asking him why people vote. Of course I want to know what his personal responses are to this question, but simultaneously I am implicated in his visions and attitudes. If my presence at times threatens him, then his words at times threaten me. I could easily dismiss these feelings on the grounds that an eleven-year-old *boy* is hardly someone to rankle a *man* of my age. But it is precisely because of everything William D. is that his words have a way of touching me.

"They vote," William D. answered, "because they want to think they have something to say in what's going on in the country. They're not even that bothered if they don't; they just want to *believe* that someone up there's listening to 'em and watching the way they vote and think. That's why. No one likes to feel he ain't part of something that's going on. So they vote. That's why *you* vote, probably, isn't it? You don't like being left out."

I recalled for William D. the tales I had heard of voting corruption in various cities. It had been uncovered and eventually accepted by people, even expected. What's a real national election without a little hanky-panky here and there? I laughed with him. A little vote-buying, a little vote-selling. Gradually I had second thoughts about what I was saying, but his look said he had heard it all a million times before.

"You know what my uncle told me?" he said in response. "He told me he once made two hundred and fifty dollars in one afternoon stuffing the voters' box. He just kept coming in again and again telling the people in charge there he was a different guy. He said he could sort of tell they knew, like, that it was the same guy coming in over and over again, but no one said anything. That's what he said anyway. He'd give 'em the names of dead people, especially those who'd just died, 'cause no one would have those guys' names crossed off yet. He said that in poor neighborhoods like around here, the records are so old that no one knows who's living and who's been dead a hundred years. That means that if they wanted to, poor folks could probably vote again and again and again. All night long if they wanted to, he said."

I explained to William D. that inadequate census records also hurt poor communities because many who might wish to vote would be unknown to voter registration officials.

"Well," he said, "I don't know. All I know is what my uncle told me. He said he voted over and over again just by changing his clothes, and that he made all that money doing it. Two hundred and fifty dollars! Something else too he said. In the old days, mostly white folks sat around in the voting places to see that everything they wanted to happen would happen all right. You know? So lots of black folks would just come in again and again knowing damn well no one could tell 'em apart." William D. told me this in perfect seriousness. Nothing else was mentioned, no humor, no embroidering the statement in any way. "He made two hundred and fifty dollars, too, just coming in and going out. They used to have tests to see whether you were intelligent enough to vote. Well, they fixed it so he didn't have to pass the test." Then, without breaking the tempo of his speech, William D. asked, "You going to vote, Tom?"

"Yes."

"For all the folks, eh?"

"Yeah."

"You going to vote for Senator Brooke?"

"Think I should tell you?" I grinned at him.

"Why not? What's the secret?"

"Well, voters have a right to privacy, you know."

"Rich ones," he muttered, "but not folks who live around here. We're supposed to be telling these people who come around here who we're voting for, and if they disagree with us they hassle us about it."

"Who? What people?"

"People coming knocking on our door. Every time there's an election they come knocking down the doors trying to make certain we're going to vote for this person or that person. My father always says he doesn't need a calendar in the house 'cause when they go knocking on the door of poor folks you know that November's got to be coming up real quick. I guess they mostly vote in November."

"Mostly."

"So, who you voting for?" He persisted.

"Brooke!"

"All right. You're a good man." He slapped my forearm and I winced. He giggled. "Hey, man," he exclaimed, "I'm really beating the shit out of you in here today, ain't I? Kicking you under the table and banging up your arm just now. What are you going to tell your old lady when you get home?"

"That I got beat up by some wild Brooke supporter."

William D. was delighted. "Tell her that. Yeah, tell her that, okay?"

How quickly he had changed from the resigned professor reporting the inevitable corruption in America's political system to a young man openly adoring a United States senator, a special senator to be sure, but someone who got there nonetheless by popular support.

"You like old Brooke, huh?"

"Yeah. I like him," William D. answered. "So you vote him in, just so the others can see that there are black folks coming. Maybe he could save a place for me too someday."

"You thinking you'd like to be a senator, William D.?"

"Maybe." He seemed somewhat uncomfortable. "I'll either be a senator or a gunman."

"A what?"

"A senator or a gunman." He wasn't smiling. "You got to get certain things done one way or the other. Somebody's got to have the power, and if I could get it, I'd like it. But if you don't have that kind of power, you got to turn to something else."

I was surprised and upset by his announcement. Whatever politics means, it stretches far out into the world for William D. and for many of his friends as well. They see or hear about the great adventures, the great takeovers and killings made by men in power. And it *is* a man's business around here. On many occasions I have heard young men of fifteen and sixteen speaking of the necessity of "having a wife so that everything looks like it's on the up and up." The language is a language of the media, the streets too, and of the homes. For the political frustrations experienced every day by the mothers and fathers of these children have to be translated into the play and work that define children's lives. Big men, then, become operators. They shove people around, not out of revenge exactly, but because that's the way even the smallest things get done. The young people around here make me believe, moreover, that each one of these big men will step on the next one if that is what advancement and progress require. But as tough as these young people sound, as truculent as they may even become, I continually hear that plaintive hope that someday a man might emerge from somewhere and make life better for everyone. It is a mystical dream, entangled surely with the verses and history of biblical writings. But it is political too, for it resides as much in Washington, Atlanta, or Hyannis as it does in Bethlehem and Judea.

William D. and I finished eating and left the restaurant. We were heading for his home on South Plaine several blocks away. He was jabbering on, a politician going through his notes, and telling me of his plans for the evening.

"Smells around here, don't it?" he interrupted himself. I nodded yes. "Got to see that old Brooke does something about that. Way I figure it is that the ecology thing's going to be fixed up where the rich folks live and then they'll send all the bad air around here. Choke us, like. Could happen. You never see the sky real blue anymore. Not like you see it in the country. It's real blue out there. That's where I'd like to live. Get me a home out there — big one, you know — and make sure no one messes up the sky. Nice green grass instead of all this dirty stuff we get down here. Have to talk to old Brooke about that."

"Or become a senator yourself." He didn't bother to comment on my remark. In the glances we exchanged lay our recognition of how foolish my words had sounded. When William D. proposes a fantasy it is permissible for me to pursue it with him, even elaborate it a bit. When I propose one, however, it seems ludicrous and out of place; and if not patronizing, then uncalled-for. Nothing etches reality more precisely for him than my playing out my own wishes and images.

"A senator?" he responded with surprise. "A gunman, more likely. Get one of those sawed-off deals and shoot the gray out of the sky. Or if I can't, then shoot the dudes who put it up there. What's the word they use for it?"

"What word?"

"I just used it," he said in frustration.

"For what?"

"You know, clean up the environment."

"Ecology," we said in unison.

"Yeah, ecology," he repeated. "Blue sky, green grass, nice house. Have one, two, three, four cars. Senator William D. Williams." He was announcing himself before a cheering mob of loyal followers. "Call me William D., folks." Peering down at the sidewalk he raised his right fist. "Power to the people," he said softly. Then he looked up at me, then forward again, and raised his fist higher and said the words more loudly and with greater energy. "Power to the people!"

Chapter 3

WHEN ADRIEN KELLER was six years old, the doctors dia-
nosed her father's lingering illness as cancer. He died
nine months later at the age of thirty-four, leaving his wife, Adrien, and three other children, two boys and a girl. Adrien
was the second-born, the first girl. Since her father Quintin's death, Adrien's mother, Sarah Clarke Keller, has taken
on two new full-time jobs in addition to her old part-time job.
Because her mother is away so much, Adrien has assumed
almost total responsibility for running the Keller household. This means that she does most of the shopping, laundry,
and cooking, as well as some of the cleaning, a chore she
shares with her older brother, Quintin Junior, and mother.
The burdens on Mrs. Keller and the two oldest children
might have been lessened had the insurance owed the family
on Quintin Keller's death been paid. For some reason,
however, it was never issued.

Adrien was eight when we met, one of several second
grade students I came to know through their teacher, Hazel
Bramore, from the Caldwell school. Knowing of my interests, Hazel introduced me to the families of these children,
and so I came to know Mrs. Keller and the other Keller children as well.

During the first years of my friendship with the Kellers,
Adrien enjoyed listening to my conversations with her
mother. She rarely said much, but we would look at one an-

other from time to time and smile. I would admire her thin gold earrings or the delicate gold necklace with the heart on it she often wore. I kidded her too about her habit of taking off her shoes the instant she entered the house, or the orange and yellow patches she sewed onto the back pocket or the knees of her jeans, or the collection of sweatshirts she was amassing.

At eleven, Adrien is a slight girl who pulls her shiny hair back tightly and clips it with colored barrettes. When she concentrates, as she does during our conversations, she oftens smoothes her hair, first on one side, then on the other. Then she pats her hair lightly on top, although by this time she is already looking at me self-consciously and grinning. She boasts of many degrees of happiness and anger, believing that each day she feels different from the day before. She is not surprised, moreover, to feel her moods change several times in the course of a few hours. She laughs freely and like her older brother hunts for the game and amusement in unusual situations. She claims to be uncomfortable during moments of silence but does not reveal her uneasiness. When I close my eyes and think of Adrien I see her smiling, a dimple forming in her right cheek, the skin around her eyes crinkling, and her hands coming up to mask her face as if she were embarrassed by something. Her mother says that the sadness that befell Adrien and her family on the death of her father has never lifted.

Adrien has a nickname, well earned, but one her brothers and sisters rarely use. Only her friends call her Glide, a name meant to describe her way of gliding from space to space like a skater. Her lovely motion is intentional, for she loves to dance. She feels free and weightless when dancing, quite the opposite of how she normally feels doing her school and home chores, although she acknowledged once that "it is already too late to get into dancing seriously. Really good dancers start when they're four and five and six."

By the time the elections drew near, Adrien and I were meeting together at least once a week, always after school, and usually in the kitchen of the Keller apartment. In time, our meetings came to be called by the entire family "Adrien's kitchen meetings." Sitting at the small rectangular table in a chair that somehow had been designated as mine, I would watch her move about the small kitchen in her stocking feet. She would push off with one foot and slide on the other to the refrigerator, all the while holding this extended position with her leg. Then she would push off with the other foot and skate to the stove, this time standing on one foot while holding the other one high behind her. Then back to the refrigerator, then to the sink, now walking with small slipping baby steps, and finally, with accentuation, falling clumsily into the chair, "her chair," opposite me.

Today would be our last "kitchen meeting" prior to the 1972 elections. Presumably, it would be a continuation of the conversation we were forced to end abruptly the week before when her younger brother, Arthur, came home from school with a bad cut. It was not a serious injury but neither of us felt like "talking politics" after seeing Arthur cry and look frightened. Still, even in her expression of concern for her brother, Adrien kept alive the political topics that interested us. Always she wished to achieve a balance between those items she wanted to discuss and those items she imagined I wanted her to discuss. At least, this had been her way in the early months of our friendship. By now, she understood that I wanted to hear whatever she wanted to tell me, and that from all these words we would discover the connections between seemingly random thoughts and the political realities of her life and the lives of the others in her family.

"I hate sickness," Adrien had said when we had finished washing and bandaging Arthur's hand and he had disappeared, still weeping, into his bedroom off the kitchen. "I get all scared inside. Sometimes, like my mother says all the time, I don't know whether I'm scared because people are really hurt, I mean seriously hurt, or because if they have to go into the hospital it may cost a lot of money. Maybe that's horrible to say." She had looked at me as if she had wanted to ask me something.

"I know about your father and the insurance policy," I told her quietly.

"I know you do," she had said. She stared at me until she could sense that I felt uneasy. "Senator Kennedy, you know, has a plan to help folks pay their hospital bills." Almost playing the role of generous host she had changed the subject for me. "Oooo-eee, that would make it wonderful. Then no one would ever have to worry, and maybe my father's money would come through. Even now, after all these years. One day a little man would come to the door — I always think this — and he'd say that he had all this money for us, all that we were supposed to get when my father died. Right? Well, if they gave me the money I just know I wouldn't spend it the way you're supposed to, like on things you need right away. I know I'd do all sorts of foolish things with it, like buy clothes I don't even need. Or presents. Someday I'd like to have a lot of money so that I could walk into someone's house and say, 'Here you go, here's a little present I bought you. Just 'cause I like you.' That'd be nice. But see, then the money wouldn't be going to where it was supposed to be going."

"But Adrien," I protested mildly, "that's well and good, but it's like saying that the powers that be might just as well *never* give you back the money 'cause it's all going to be wasted."

My words angered her, but she was unable to respond with the force that I could see building up within her.

"I ain't saying *that!* I ain't saying that at all. We want that money! Ain't anyone got the right to hold it from us anymore. What I'm saying is that it's hard to keep hoping when you see the way they treat us. That's what I'm saying. That money doesn't have anything to do with my father anymore. It's the city, the government. They're using it for other things, things that will make *them* money, not us. I ain't saying we don't deserve it." She placed her hands on the edge of the table as if she might have wanted to shove it over onto me. "I'm just trying to hold on to some hope, that's all, but all those politicians and funny little people working in those offices downtown, they're just playing their little games. They're jiving us. What do they care? It's no skin off their backs. So what do they care?"

There was no need for me to respond; no gratuitous "comforting" to be offered. There was nothing, moreover, about Adrien's anger that carried with it the plea to feel something special, or to rescue her from something, a fantasy, admittedly, I often entertain. When her anger arises I not only feel our friendship more intensely, I feel, selfishly, that we have hit on critical issues, critical themes, but she must lead both of us on from here.

Health care as an abstract issue was clearly a political concern for her, but the matter of her father's death and the changes that have taken place in her family are even more important. I watched her closely, admiring two rings she wore that had been made from baby spoons, and wondered whether speaking with me was burden enough without the reminders of the sad days years ago. Why is it that children seem to be less aware than adults of the act of dying? At certain ages they appear not to understand the concept of death at all, although by four they know the difference between living things and dead things, or what they might call "not real" things. They know, too, that imagined objects and people must be distinguished from living and dead objects. They understand the significance of the body and the value of health. They fear hurt, mutilation, disease. They grimace in front of the television set and in movies when doctors and dentists probe and stick and jab. Children much older than Adrien cry in the emergency rooms of the City Hospital from fright even more than from pain.

But in the community in which Adrien lives, the children are also aware of the ways in which laws, rights, regulations, and the lack of money affect the illnesses and injuries they and their families sustain, and death as well. Throughout their lives they have heard the stories of children dying from illnesses that only rarely put rich children in hospitals, and they have known some of these children. They may not be familiar with words like "tonsillectomy," "meningitis," "epilepsy," "colitis," "herniation," but most of the children know people who became ill because of inadequate medical treatment. This they tell me without any particular bitterness. Nor do they dress up their stories in the language of politics or popular political rhetoric. "If we had more money, we might have got the drugs faster," they say. Or "We waited so long for the doctor to come out into the waiting room by the time he did it was already too late." They are aware of the realities of medical service but seemingly hold no one responsible for the inadequate care they and their families receive. "Jonesy ate so much candy his teeth fell out," I heard William D. proclaim once, unaware that the boy, David Jones, had never once in his life — and he was fifteen — visited a dentist.

Nonetheless, issues like medical insurance, low salaries,

rising prices, rising rents, inability to employ doctors and lawyers, young people like Adrien and William D. understand only too well. How they connect these issues to something as abstract as a political system is a problem one often ignores or deems irrelevant in light of the injustices and daily hurts they endure. Many children in this community continue to try to understand exactly how government agencies and politicians function, and how laws affect the people of the city or the nation, and what influence a President can have on the people. This connection of personal events to the concept of a political system is encouraged in school and at home, and probably with Adrien and William D. by me as well. The search, however, for the connection goes on, which means that these children want to be able to transcend personal family experiences and incorporate rudimentary ideas of political theory and philosophy.

Adrien moved gracefully about the kitchen, pouring tea for me. At the sink she fetched a clean plate, then handed me the cup of tea without saying anything.

"Beautiful," I said before tasting it.

"Try it first."

I sipped the tea. "It's perfect. Why don't you have some?"

"Never. I can't stand it. Tea's awful. No one here drinks it. I like chocolate milk best but we never get it."

"Just as well," I said. "It rots your teeth."

Adrien just looked at me. "Well, let's see," she said at last, "what are we going to talk about today?" There was a studied quality about her question.

"Whatever you think is important."

"Abortion!" She had been waiting for me to say, Let's get to work.

"What?"

"Abortion," she repeated, sitting down in the chair across from me. "You know what abortion is, don't you?"

"Yeah. I've heard of it." We smiled at one another.

"I think they ought to have no abortion laws anywhere," she began. "Anybody who wants one should get one. And they should be real cheap too, and safe. That's the most important thing, they have to be safe."

"Performed by doctors, you mean?"

"In the beginning anyway." She was thinking about my question, her eyes squinting slightly. Her slim hands pushed against the edge of the enamel table. "But pretty soon they should have other people learning how to do them too. Lots of girls are really getting into trouble around here, so they better do something soon."

"Do the girls you go to school with talk about things like abortion?"

"Sometimes. Not always. But like, the other day, a group of us were talking to this one girl who's pregnant. She was in grammar school with us but now she doesn't go to school anymore. She's pregnant and doesn't want to have the baby. I don't blame her. I can't even imagine what it's like to be pregnant. She looked so strange. We saw her coming and I almost started to laugh. So did Cynthia, my girl friend, you know. Cynthia Willingham? I mean, here was Marlene walking down the street with her sneakers and high green socks, and she couldn't even button this leather coat she was wearing. She looked like she was going to fall over, like she had an elephant inside her." Adrien began to giggle. Putting her hand up to her mouth, she looked at me for forgiveness. I was grinning. She slapped her forehead with the heel of her hand in order to regain her composure but it didn't work and she exploded with laughter.

"She looked so funny. Like one half of her was girl, you

know, and the other half was real old. An old lady. Half girl, half lady, and she's supposed to have a baby any week now, I guess. But boy, was she ever frightened by it."

"What's her boy friend say?" I wondered. Adrien was calming down. My question caused her to stop laughing.

"Freddie's a pig!" she announced bitterly. "No one sees him. He told his friend, this other kid, that she should get an abortion, but he never stopped to think that you can't get one so easy. You got to have a lot of money for it."

I watched her closely, recalling accounts of women wanting abortions and the unnecessary humiliation and despair that so often accompany this operation. "But why the hell aren't they more careful?" several women in this same community have asked me when we spoke about it. "Why don't they behave like they're supposed to? Twelve, thirteen, fourteen years old, going around with just any man they find," Mrs. Evelyn Botsworth, who lives four blocks away on McCall Street, said one morning.

Evelyn Botsworth is an old friend of mine, one of the first people I met in the neighborhood when I began working here eight years ago. More often than not, I end up at her home after my "official interviewing sessions" are completed, a fact she often jokes about with me. "When are you going to interview *me?*" she asks all the time. "My God, I can tell you just as much as all these other folks can. Next time you get those kids of yours going on some big topic, come by here and I'll tell you what Evelyn thinks about it."

This is exactly what I did when the matter of abortion arose with some young people several weeks before my talk with Adrien. I went to the Botsworth home and notified Evelyn that the time had finally arrived. I had come to *interview* her.

"No more messing around with you, Mrs. Evelyn Botsworth." I grinned. "Here's the question of the morning."

"Seems to me," she answered curtly, "there's no issue here at all, and no reason in the world why abortion has to be part of the election campaigns. If a girl's old enough to be doing those things, then she'll have to pay the price that God puts on an act like that. Nerve of all these girls and boys thinking they can just behave like they do."

I disagreed with Evelyn, although I turned out to have a rather weak argument. My position was that many young people are careful but have not learned of contraceptives and caution and all the rest. I even tried to relate the act of abortion to politics. "It's easier, remember, Evelyn, for richer kids to cover up their acts. If someone has a little money you can help your daughter out. If a family can't scrape it together to see a dentist a couple of times a year, not to mention get the right sort of gynecological examinations for their daughters, then how can anyone expect them to have money lying around for an expensive abortion?"

Evelyn Botsworth remained firm. She was a big strong woman who walked in a way that caused her weight to shift from side to side. Her breathing came with difficulty, but not her smile. Still, she was tough and, on this one point, adamant.

"I can dig your politics, M.I.T.," she said, "but don't you go messing with *my* religion. You ain't going to get me on this one. A girl's got to be careful, particularly now. In my day if a girl got pregnant, she got married or had that child, if she was lucky, and that took care of that. But these girls today, even the ones in your friend Adrien Keller's class — and don't go thinking children that small ain't messing around with one another every chance they get — just want to have their fun. They don't want responsibility. They don't want to be nailed down to some place. They just want freedom. So what I say is that this abortion thing belongs nowhere in politics. I don't want to hear it in their speeches, not even if Old Shirley's running for the House. I can't listen to what that Nixon fellow has to say, but abortion ain't his bag. Shouldn't be either." Laughing and wheezing, she patted her chest to get air. "Ain't his bag. McGovern's neither. War, money, food prices, 'specially those prices, day-care centers, and jobs, 'specially for our people, but abortion? No ma'am." She sang the words. "Uh-uh. That's private business."

Rather than say something I let her know my frustration in the way I turned toward her as if to speak, and shook my head slightly from side to side. Walking all the while, Evelyn pretended she had noticed nothing. At last she spoke, but never once did she look over at me.

"Now, now, don't you go wagging your head at me," she warned. "You asked me whether you could ask some questions. I told you yes if it doesn't interfere with my work and general carrying on. You didn't say anything about *arguing* with me. This here's no political debate, so you hold your head from wagging." She was having trouble breathing and I put my arm around her. "Shoo, this cold air's so bad for me. It's just plain mean out here. Get me to Florida, Lord. Transport me to Miami Beach, and leave all your abortion talk up North with the professor here. Amen."

Adrien Keller's attitudes on abortion hardly coincided with Evelyn Botsworth's. Many of Adrien's friends shared her views, but many too would have sided with Evelyn. The arguments over the right of women to have abortions, the few, that is, that I have heard in this community, focus on religious principles and methods of contraception. The women invoke their rights and God's rights, and appeal to a sort of social philosophy, but references to political aspects of the arguments are always forthcoming. It is in the context of being a woman that discussions on abortion more naturally fit. Sexuality, the possibility of becoming pregnant, the wish to be pregnant, the fear of illness or discomfort, the fascination with babies, the chance perhaps to leave school for a while, if not forever, the jokes about scaring a boy friend with the news that one is pregnant, the imagined and real reactions of parents, siblings, boy friends, and finally marriage, separation, and divorce, all form the background of these discussions. And there is at least one thing more: the recognition of the role of mother and the presence in these women's lives of that one woman. And after her come the not-so-abstract political factors.

"Here's the way I feel about it," Adrien resumed. "Sure, a person's religion plays an important part, and so does what their family thinks. But there are just some things that people need the government for, even when the government isn't that fair, which is a lot of the time. See, if they don't make any laws, then we're going to be in lots of trouble. Rich families don't need to have a lot of laws. They'll do what they have to do anyway. But poor people . . ." She looked embarrassed suddenly, fearing that I should see her family as being poor.

". . . If we don't have laws to protect us," she was saying, "then we don't really have very much. Like at school. If there's a law that says we *have* to be given hot food with our lunches, then they have to give it to us whether they like to or not, 'cause the law says they have to."

"But aren't there times, Adrien, when the law says they *have* to but they still don't give what they promised?"

"I guess so," she answered quietly. "I guess that's right." She seemed perplexed by my words, but lack of sophistication about political and legal processes was not what put her on the defensive. Of course she knew the emptiness of laws as opposed to, say, the almost sacrosanct nature of school and home rules and regulations. She understood, moreover, that laws by themselves guarantee nothing, or at least to her family very little. If her father's death had taught her one thing, it was that laws can be bent and guarantees twisted out of shape until they are unrecognizable; until they need not be honored.

It was not an intellectual confusion, therefore, or a contradiction that momentarily silenced Adrien. It was hope, a single thread of hope that I had snapped with my question. If laws could not do it for her — bring hot lunches, guarantee jobs, good schools, insurance money, adequate health care, retirement benefits, and reasonable salaries and prices — then what under God could? If laws could not underwrite personal safety and well-being, and a father isn't around to do it, and a mother works three jobs merely to make survival possible, and the rich, as she believes, don't bother with laws that aren't written in ways that benefit them, then what is anyone left with? What do I believe in if laws cannot be trusted? lay behind Adrien Keller's confused expression.

Adrien continued to look puzzled. She stared at me before speaking again.

"I guess I want laws to make a difference but I know that they don't. Or else, it takes so long for them to . . . to . . ."

"Institute them?" I offered.

"Yeah. Make them come true. I think kids want to believe in the law, and the government too. We keep going back to it. I mean, nobody I know *really* questions it that seriously. Nobody's really ever going to be able to change it. Lots of kids will say we have to be represented in it. Even if we don't have the vote, we have to have our say. But I worry whether we would help in the right way. Do you know what I mean?"

Chapter 4

EVERY DAY that I am with Adrien I am moved by her words, her concerns, her feelings about the everyday moments of life, and what in these moments is marked for her. Adrien's spirit and personality are always evident in her knowledge of politics. But it is more than political sophistication that she and William D., too, possess. It is an adult posture, an approach of intelligence, not just "ghetto savvy," maturity and courage — an approach, strangely, that often makes me feel uncomfortable. Sitting in the kitchen, listening to her talk about abortion, health care, the meaning of laws, the perpetual grayness of the sky, the smells in her neighborhood, or her list of chores for that one evening, causes me to wonder about children, rich and poor, who cannot just be children, but who early on assume adult responsibilities. I think sometimes that ironically one of the many rights not granted to children is the right to be a child. While I may be put off when William D. rushes for a restaurant booth without thinking about who will order and pay, I am later relieved that this childlike thoughtlessness remains in him.

The matter, however, is more complex, for no one can prove the ill effects of children assuming adult roles "too early" in their lives. Indeed, Adrien's and William D.'s daily responsibilities probably increase their sense of competence and worth. So it is not a question of forced maturity as much as it is the ill effect of poverty on children. The realities of busing or abortion cannot possibly hurt these children as much as the enduring realities of poverty and the lack of rights. Debates on any political issue only make them politically more aware.

Still, the most fundamental of all images of self arise in my political discussions with these two children. The arguments they hear and read about at times make them question themselves, their talents and capacities, if not their destiny. Watching Adrien, I will argue with myself that the most idyllic and love-filled setting of childhood, a setting that has not yet been perpetuated in adult society, be maintained for as long as possible. For within this setting, self-love, narcissism, pride, confidence, whatever one chooses to call it, is harvested. Human will is born in this setting too, a will that later on can combat the feeling that one is lacking in some way, as well as the feelings of self-doubt.

Yet again, the issue of poverty affects this development of the will. For children like Adrien and William D., who have in their short lives received great quantities of love, have known nothing that resembles an idyllic setting where free play is possible day in and day out. And while their own style of play and work has developed in them wills of firmness as well as resiliency, they will be hard pressed, as the years go on, to combat feelings of self-doubt which almost every social institution will instill in them. Even as adults, when they will articulate the deadly effects of racism and poverty, they will continue to feel the sudden sharp pains of self-doubt and wonder: What might have become of me had I been better or stronger? As much as political issues are conceptualized or made into sociological abstractions, they are also personalized, taken by the child into his heart of hearts. But with Adrien there is always that other thing that I cannot ever shake from my mind: it is her searching for a way to express her grief.

I sense that Adrien is content to have our friendship be based on my original research intentions. She knows that I visit her home to seek information and share ideas and experiences with her and her family. She is aware, naturally, that she, more than anyone else in the family, is the focus of my work, and this is satisfactory with her. She also recognizes the extent and limitations of this work, and how its final product might matter to her. Still, she has never said, "Now that you know about us, why don't you do something about it?" It is enough, apparently, to recount events and experiences. Either that or she is resigned, realizing that no one she knows will ever help to effect change. If I tell her about personal experiences, that is acceptable to her, even pleasurable, but nothing more is expected of me. At least that is what I detect. What she tells her friends and her mother about me and our work behind my back is something else, and I know that she does tell them things.

Some remarks about the research, of course, filter back to me through the children's parents. Trying hard to separate her feelings about the work from her feelings about me and about politics generally, Mrs. Williams once said: "The goal, I think, is not that people have to get to the point of being colorblind. No one needs to tell me you're white, and no one needs to tell you I'm black. If we can't see that, we can't be too much up here." She placed her fingers along the side of her head. "The goal is simpler than that. You get to know our family, we get to know you and your family. That they aren't equal, well, that's what we're all going to have to live with. Maybe together we'll change it. But right now I know it matters to William D., and Adrien Keller too, that you come. So keep coming. Only don't you try to teach them lots of things. Let them be teaching you. If that goes along with the kind of research you're doing, I can approve. Let them teach you, and let them, kind of, change you. That part of it may be even more important. There has to be change, and it only comes when someone's listening. So this time, you do the listening. Don't you go lecturing them.

"Folks that always go talking at you aren't folks who respect the way you're living. They got all kinds of ideas in their heads about the way you *should* be living your life; telling children how to act and what to think and all." She paused for a moment. "Course the silent ones can be just as dangerous, I suppose, sitting there listening to you tell them what you're feeling inside. I see 'em sitting there so polite and nice in the school meetings, then the next month comes and they go on making their plans and starting all their programs as though they hadn't been listening to you at all. You should see some of them. They're looking at you, suffering with you, it seems, to look at their faces. Fact is, I go home sometimes thinking I've really impressed those men, changed a few of their minds too. That will be the last time they'll go thinking those old thoughts or singing those old songs, I'll say to myself. Then the next month, there they are again, with the same old songs and the same old politics. I haven't changed them one small bit. It's all been a waste. A big, ugly waste. And there I am, with my husband telling me I'm just wasting everybody's time, especially my own, planning on going back there the next time they meet and start the same old thing all over again."

I said nothing. How does one respond to such a statement? Keep trying, life isn't always filled with futile attempts. Do I tell her not to feel humiliated when she gives so much of herself and sees with her own eyes that her words and actions have had little effect on anyone?

"Maybe poor folks," she concluded ironically, "are dumber than other folks." She looked away and wrinkled up her eyes. "Maybe they are. No one with any intelligence would keep doing what I'm doing, month in, month out at those meetings and not quit. Lordy, those men in the City Hall and the Federal Building downtown, they must think we're really dumb in this community. They must really think we're pretty awful dumb."

Adrien was finishing her report to me. She glanced at the clock several times, concerned whether preparations for dinner had to get underway. I started to leave but she insisted that we still had time. I knew that the moment I left she would be scurrying around in the small kitchen, working mechanically on making dinner, and playing over in her head what she had told me, and what she might have been prompted to tell but never did. How one speaks to children is part of the political dilemma each of us faces, for it touches upon the issue of children's rights. What children choose to divulge to us and what they choose to keep inside themselves forever is another part of the dilemma.

"You know the Miltons who live across the street?" she asked suddenly.

"No."

"Well, Willy Milton — you don't know him?" Her voice sounded childlike.

"No, I'm sorry. I don't know any Willy Milton," I repeated,

"Well, anyway, I thought you did. His family moved. Not because they wanted to, but because the city decided they wanted the apartment where he lived."

"Urban renewal."

"Yeah." I heard her bitterness. "Renewal. They told the Miltons that they didn't have to go right away if they didn't want to, you know."

"Appeal it, you mean?"

"If that's what you call it. They gave 'em an office in the Government Center to call. So they called and called and called. Every day. They spoke to the people there and the people even came to their house to look around."

"But they moved 'em out anyway," I anticipated her story.

"Moved 'em? They *threw* 'em out. They had more lawyers coming around there telling 'em they had no rights for this or that. You should have seen all the lawyers they had. That's the government for you."

"They relocate them?" I asked.

"No, they did not," she answered defiantly. "Nobody helped them move. My brother Quintin and me, we helped them a little. They gave us dinner at their house 'cause they appreciated what we did for them. But they never got a penny neither. Promises though. They got lots of those."

Adrien had never before mentioned the Miltons' forced move. She and her friends, however, often inspect the property where the Miltons lived. Some two and a half years later, the building still stands. It has not yet been gutted and the children cannot figure out why, if the Miltons were made to leave, the city did not immediately use the site.

"What was their hurry is what I'd like to know." She was saying. "They threw 'em out so fast, why didn't they take the building over and do something with it? One minute they need it so badly, but now it's two years, more even, and it's still there. You can see it if you want to. You want to see it sometime?"

"I believe you, Adrien. I'm sure you're right."

"What's very sad about that building," Adrien was saying, "is that every time we go anywhere near that block with

Willy, he makes us walk by so we can look at the house. So we'll go there too, like we do all the time, and Willy gives this stupid little speech of his. Like, he'll point up at the different windows and say, 'You see that one in the corner on the third floor?'" Adrien mimicked Willy's excitement. " 'Well, that was my brother's room. My room didn't have a window so you can't see it. It's over there somewhere.' " She pointed up toward the kitchen ceiling and I found myself following her hand. Seeing my eyes move she began to laugh. "Up there," she teased. "In the crack. That's Willy's room. No, really, he does this all the time. Every time we go there. 'This is my brother's room, and that's the living room, and that's this room' and on and on. It's really a big drag being there with him."

"Can you talk about it with him?" I proposed.

"Well, we would," she began almost apologetically, "except that when he's saying this he always starts to cry. Always. And it makes the rest of us feel so bad to see this kid crying that we feel we can't say anything to him. So we don't."

"I think you're wise."

"Well, I don't know about if we're wise, but when a kid's crying 'cause he misses his house and there isn't any reason that anyone can find out why they didn't do anything with the house, then it'd shake a lot of other people up too. You know what I mean? Like someone was saying they should blow it up with a bomb. I don't think that's so good, using a bomb, but if the Miltons can't live there, and if the city says they have to get out, then they should either put other families in there or use the building in some way that helps the people in the community. But it's just sitting there. It's just sitting there like they wanted to show the Miltons and the rest of us how strong they could be if they wanted to. I don't think it's fair, that's all."

Gradually, Adrien's manner relaxed, and the apartment seemed quiet again.

"We went down to those government offices once. I remember my mother took us. They listened to us. They made us think we really had rights. But you can see what we got. Nothing!" She gestured with her hands in a manner to take in the kitchen and living room. "You can see it with your own eyes. You can sit right where you are and look from one end of our house to the other. That's what we got all right. They ain't never going to come across.

"When I listen to all these politicians — like tonight on television, they'll be on with all their foolish commercials; vote for this one, vote for that one, don't vote for McGovern because he changes his mind and don't vote for whoever." Her tone was sarcastic and irritable. "I could throw up. It's true. They don't have the slightest idea about people's feelings. They go on doing whatever they like just as long as it helps *them*. But they don't care whether people are made unhappy by what they do, and all the laws they pass. They don't care. Why should *they* care? They don't throw rich folks out of their houses. Someday I'm going to take a photograph of that kid standing in front of the house where they threw him out of, and send it to all the senators. All of them!" She hesitated. "Did you ever see that picture in the paper of the girl with her back on fire?"

"The Vietnamese girl?"

"Yeah. That's the one."

"Hmm."

"They put it up in school on the bulletin board. We talked about it in class too. The teacher asked us how many people here think this photograph will really help to, like, change the government's mind about dropping all those bombs?"

"What happened?"

"One girl raised her hand." Adrien's body stiffened in the chair with excitement. "She thought that Nixon was going to look at that picture and say, 'I've got to stop. Stop the bombs, man. Kids are getting hurt. Can't have that.'" She sounded imperious, dictatorial even. "Then the teacher asked how many people felt they'd drop the bombs anyway? We all put our hands up, except that one girl." Adrien shook her head angrily. "They don't care about kids. They say they do, but they don't. Anyway, it's easier to say you like kids in those commercials. That don't mean a thing. You can just say you're for kids and everybody will have to vote for you. But someday I'd like to send them that picture of Willy crying out there on Temple Street."

For several moments Adrien and I stared at one another. I didn't need to remind her that she herself had argued for the futility of reaching congressmen or changing their minds with photographs of burning children.

It is tempting for me to draw connections between political figures and parents. How easy it would be to interpret Adrien's involvement with the Milton boy, and the boy's own sense of loss, in terms of her own losses, political, personal, and otherwise. Why after all, I could argue, would she remind *me* of the money owed her family and then go off into a discussion of a boy who pines for the loss of his first home? Surely there are all sorts of associations to be drawn in all of this. Is there, for example, something to be made of her bitterness toward the campaign commercials? Does that bitterness relate to me? Does she link my interest in children to the candidates' interest in children, and lump us all together under the heading "perfunctory involvement"?

With Adrien calming down, it was I who felt anger. How

infuriating to be forced out of your home and have your belongings dropped in some strange apartment. And then,
without being able to appeal this action to anyone, you are
reminded every day that no one lives in what you still consider to be your home, which must mean that no reason un-
derwrote the relocation in the first place. The action of evic-
tion angers and terrifies me; it is an unequivocal statement
of power and domination; one can only feel helplessness.

"We told our teachers about the Miltons. Mr. McEachern
said that we should keep going and find out all we could and
report back. So Pigeon, you don't know her, she goes and
tries to find out. Well, you can imagine, they wouldn't tell
her anything. Can you see this little girl, like me, walking
into an office of the government and asking the man there,
'Can you tell me please what you plan to do with the building on the corner of Temple and South Plaine?' Can you
see it?" Adrien began to giggle. "Know what I told her? I
said, 'Pigeon, you're crazy if you think you're ever going to
learn anything. First off, they don't want no children pester-
ing them around there while they're doing their work.
Next, they don't have to tell you anything. And after that,
you got to learn to speak like an important lawyer.' William
D., you know, always says he's going to be a senator; maybe I
should be a lawyer and learn to talk like those big shots."

"Why not?" I suggested seriously.

"Why not what?"

"You become —"

"Me become a lawyer?" she interrupted with a surprised
tone. "Me? I'm too dumb to be a lawyer. And besides, who
ever heard of a girl lawyer?"

Now it was I who was incredulous. "Adrien, don't you
know about women lawyers?"

"No, I don't," she answered flatly.

"Really?"

"Really. They got 'em?"

"They got 'em? Sure they got 'em. You really don't know?"

"No. I really don't. I ain't kidding with you, Tom. I don't know any girl lawyers."

"There are. There are."

"Well, I'll be . . ." She began to laugh. "I really didn't know. This is the first I heard of it. Honest to God."

Adrien's hands lay palms up on the table like a supplicant's. We looked at one another, both of us, strangely, on the verge of smiling, maybe even laughing out loud for some reason. I wanted to tell her that she was too smart not to know about women lawyers. I don't like to face the areas of ignorance of certain people, indeed the very word "ignorance" is dangerous and misleading. Perhaps I thought about the unevenness of Adrien's information about our culture and what parts of this culture she can take as her own. She knows things that people older and "better educated" don't know, and she knows these things because she has learned them, not simply because she has experienced them. But here was something that she didn't know, namely that women can become lawyers. That a culture evolves to the point where an enormous segment of the population is deprived of the chance to pursue a life's work is criminal enough. But that these forces cause people not even to know what they are being deprived of leaves one utterly dumfounded and exasperated. I guess, Adrien, I was about to say, we're both uninformed about some things. We both have areas of ignorance, and mine are just as significant as yours.

Then suddenly, as if she were reading my mind and feeling my reactions, she began to nod her head and pat my hand very gently. "We're both learning something today, aren't we?" she said.

"We certainly are."

"You're learning about urban renewal, I hope. Why don't they put that into the campaign?" Adrien questioned me.

"I don't know. I think in fact they —"

"You know what they do, the mayors and those people? They say the cities are dying. Then they go and ask the main government in Washington for money. At least that's what I heard."

"Revenue sharing." I felt like a fool continually supplying titles and labels for processes she knew about full well. But my interventions didn't faze her in the slightest.

"So they get the money and what do they do? They fix up the cities where *they* live, not where *we* live. Any minute we can get a letter that says we have to move too. So we'd have to go. Maybe to a project or some other place. Maybe it would be better, but if it's like the Miltons' it won't be. They have two less rooms in their new place now and they have to pay more rent. That's what you call urban renewal. I think it's a crime what they do to families. It's like murder. Mr. Milton was so upset about it, you should have seen. Willy said they had to put him in the hospital to settle his nerves. He had to take this special medicine too. I couldn't believe it, but when I tried to think what I might do if they made us move like that, it made sense to me. I think I'd go crazy too if they did it to us."

"The government could help." I sighed.

"They could but they won't, and everybody knows why."

For the moment there seemed to be nothing we had to say to one another. Both of us were a trifle uncomfortable, sitting across the table from each other. Adrien looked suddenly behind her, checking to see if she had left some perishables in the sink. I was sitting upright, searching in my pocket for a note with someone's telephone number on it. Then we were starting at one another again, and listening to the soft noises in the kitchen.

Something about the way she was sitting made me believe she did not want me to leave, that she had more to tell. I waited. Being young, she honored the code that adults excuse children, but the manner of her self-consciousness was an invitation to ask her to speak. "I know it's getting late," I began, "but is there . . ."

"I was thinking about those commercials again." Her voice was low and flat.

"The candidates?"

"Yeah. Those ones."

"Thinking about me too?" I asked timidly.

"You? No. Why should I be thinking of you? You supposed to be running for some office?" She waved her hand playfully in my direction.

"No, I'm not running for anything, but I was thinking maybe my interest in you makes you think about the candidates' interest in children generally."

She looked perplexed. "You want to run that one by me again?"

"I don't think so." I laughed.

"Your interest in kids and Nixon's interest in kids?" she questioned me with all the incredulity she could muster.

"Yeah. Something like that."

"You got to be kidding, man. He doesn't even *know* children. I'm not even so sure he knows his *own* children. The way you see 'em together makes you wonder just a little bit, doesn't it?"

" 'Cause they don't touch a lot, you mean?"

"Touch?" she came back with feigned surprise. "They

don't even talk. You see that man when he came back from Russia? He kissed his family like he was on his way to the kitchen for a drink of water instead of just back from traveling all the way around the world. Touch 'em? Whew, he's something else, that man. He really is."

Many children have said much the same thing about the President. Some, being younger than Adrien and William D., naturally know less about political issues and how these issues are played out in their communities. But even these children have commented occasionally on the President's conservative manner. Senator McGovern, they felt, appeared warmer, more open, and in a way touchable. "He needs a grandchild," a ten-year-old remarked to me the day before the elections. "That Nixon, man, needs a grandchild."

"Well, what were you thinking just then, Adrien? Would you share it?"

"Oh yeah, sure. About the commercials for the President, you mean?"

"Whatever it was."

"Well, I guess I was daydreaming just a little. Every once in a while I pretend that I'm the President's wife."

"Pat Nixon?"

"Not really her exactly, but just any President's wife, you know." Adrien was not at all embarrassed by what she was saying. "And I'm in the White House with a whole mess of servants, having dinner parties for all kinds of famous folks, and listening to all the big important decisions being made. Maybe I'll arrange to have my daughter get married so everybody could see her there. And I'm traveling around like they get to do. I'd do that. Be here, then there. I'd have my own plane, just me and the President like you always see them. And living in that big house with all those rooms, and having all my friends from school and around here coming to Washington to visit us. That's where the White House is, in Washington, right?"

"Yes. Right."

"Yeah, that's what I thought. Only I thought someone was saying that it really is in Virginia or someplace."

"No, it's in Washington, D.C."

"But Washington isn't a real state. Right?"

"Right. It's a district. But you're right. It's not a state."

"Yeah." Her dream was alive again. "So all these kids are tramping through the White House wanting to see me, so in I come, marching right into this big room I imagine they got there with gold carpets, with this beautiful dress on, everything matching up real perfect, you know, and all the people are sort of swooning when they see me. 'Mrs. President,' they say." Adrien was starting to giggle. "And they're bowing down, like I was the queen or something. Thing that makes me nervous is I always get to the part where they make me give a little talk, you know, in front of all those folks. Oh, wow, do I ever get the shakes thinking about *that*. I get nervous every day talking in my class, so I guess I don't qualify to be the Mrs. President." She paused. "That and a few other things. Might be nice, though, for a while," she added wistfully. "I heard that Mrs. Nixon was really poor when she was my age. That's right, isn't it? I read that, I think."

"I think she was poor when she was young." I thought of the phrase "coming from humble origins."

"Well, if she made it, then I might too. Probably win the lottery before that would happen though." She moved in the chair in a way that suggested she wished to shrug off the fantasy and be separated from it. "That's a silly thought, I know," she continued, "but I do have one like it that's more serious."

"Which is?"

"Which is that I pretend Martin Luther King is the President and Mrs. King is his wife. I mean, I know she's his wife, was his wife, I'm getting so confused. I pretend," she started again, and more slowly this time, "that Martin Luther King is the President, and Mrs. King is the President's wife. That's all."

"And?"

"Nothing. Everything's just real nice, that's all." She tilted her head to one side. "They have nice children, too, and he's not afraid to be close to them. You know what I mean? Touch them and give them big hugs. President King," she mused aloud. "President Martin Luther King. Do you know what Mrs. King's first name is?"

"Coretta," I answered dutifully.

"Coretta, right. Mrs. Coretta King. Mrs. Adrien King. Mrs. Coretta Keller. Hey, that's pretty close. King, Keller. Keller, King. K, K. My head's going weak on me."

A few minutes later we stopped. Adrien was talking half to herself about food for dinner and tomorrow's school work. Our conversation, she reminded me, had kept her from starting her homework assignments, and now she would have to work especially hard and quickly in order to be in bed at the hour her mother demanded. As we walked toward the front door she laughingly suggested that she would write a paper for English on the elections and her daydreams, only she said her teacher would never accept it. We stopped at the front door and she started to help me with my coat, but then withdrew her hand.

"I like talking about these things," she said.

"Me too."

I think at that instant Adrien would have liked it had I kissed her good-bye. We had both been uplifted by her fantasy; we had both rejoiced in her images and the trip we had taken together. In her way of recounting the fantasy, she had allowed me to enter it. It was ours, a poem she had shared with no one else, and now as we both tried to come down from a feeling of being transcendent and subdue our exhilaration, I wanted to say to an audience somewhere, "I'm the man who accompanied Adrien Keller to Washington."

"Adrien," I began as she unlatched the door chain, "I have one more question. I wonder, do you think kids your age, like you, should have the chance to vote?"

"Me? Vote? Are you kidding?" She was incredulous. "Vote? Heck no! We shouldn't vote. I wouldn't know what to do. Adults vote, not kids. We don't know anywhere near enough to vote for anything, except for those elections in school."

"Would you *like* to vote, though?" I persisted.

"Sure," she replied. "Someday I'm going to vote." She sounded like a little girl proclaiming that someday she would grow big and tall. "When I'm old enough, but not now. I'm still too young. Anyway, if the adults know what they're doing, kids don't have to vote."

"I was just wondering," I said, heading for the stairs and wrestling with my coat. "Take care, Adrien."

"Yeah. You too. Don't you get lost now going home." She was grinning.

Chapter 5

SARAH KELLER, Adrien's mother, a tall, thin, handsome woman of forty-two, had never heard Adrien's fantasy about being the President's wife. Nor had she heard her daughter's attitudes on abortion, her description of the Miltons being moved, or the pain felt by Adrien when she talked about dislocation and loss. But Mrs. Keller did recall each of her children coming to her on many occasions wondering whether they were going to have to move. She remembered, too, that her children's questions were filled more with fear than excitement, but never did the family sit down and talk about why the government takes over certain buildings and relocates one family here and another one there, and why evacuated buildings remain empty for so long. She recognized, however, the value in having her children listen in on political talk:

"Rich folks may not need to pass these things on to their children, but around here everybody has to be smart. What they really ought to be teaching in school is law. That's what the children need to know: Their rights! Everybody has to know their rights. It sure seems more important to me that they learn that than all the mathematics they're forced to learn in school. What do poor folks have that much of that they have to learn to count anyway?"

When her husband was alive, Sarah Keller augmented the family's income by working thirty hours a week in the kitchen of a downtown bakery shop. Upon his death after almost two years of hospitalization, and left with medical bills but little insurance money, she took on a second thirty-hour-a-week job as a waitress in a restaurant across the street from the bakery shop. When even this much work failed to yield the income she needed, Mrs. Keller became a cleaning woman in an office building three nights a week. Finishing work at midnight or two in the morning, she often sleeps downtown rather than coming home. It is not uncommon for her working and sleeping schedules to keep her from seeing her children for as many as four days at a stretch.

"It just works out that way," she told me one warm afternoon as I waited for Adrien to return from school. "You'd think for all the millions of hours my husband worked, and for all the millions of dollars they get in taxes and all their other deals, and what they got from *our* paying *our* taxes, that I could get a break somehow. I'm sorry you're only going to be writing about the children. Well, I'm not sorry," she said, turning to look at me. "But some of us older folks have one helluva time making it through too, you know. I hear lots of folks at work saying that you have to have faith in the generation coming up. I'd like to believe that. All my kids are going to be in that generation. But why would anyone be thinking they're going to have it any easier? Take a look at my Adrien. She never complains and she's been the mother in this house since the time she was six. He died soon after her seventh birthday, I guess it was. Two days later we ate a cake I brought home from the bakery, and the next day she went to work, making us dinners, cleaning the house, tending to the smaller children. Now, what chance has she got? But what else could I do? There isn't anything anyone can do. I've got no family. The family I have left is all in the South still. Mississippi, Georgia,

Florida too, I think. God only knows where they are now. You believe that I'm not even certain whether my grandparents are still alive? How does a person find out?" she asked no one in particular.

"Look here at his photograph." Mrs. Keller handed me a framed photograph of her husband. In it Mr. Keller stands with his right arm around his wife, who looks much younger than she does now although not that many years have elapsed, and with his left arm on the shoulder of his oldest son who stands in front of his parents looking directly at the camera. "He was a real gentleman," Mrs. Keller was saying. "God must have wanted him awfully badly to strike him down at that early age. Awfully badly." We studied the photograph together, side by side. I said nothing. Finally she took it gently from me and set it back on the table, precisely where it had stood before. "Men always take the pictures," she lamented. "We have hundreds of me and just one or two of him. The children are very unhappy about this. They miss him. They wish I had more photographs. What do I tell them?" It was only then that she looked away from the photograph.

I watched her shift her body around so that she could scan the room and check on her other belongings, her property. This is what I have left in my life, I imagined her thinking. The little that is in this room, and my children. We looked at the gray dust that had collected on the tables and on the shelves between the two front windows. At the shelves' edges its accumulation was so heavy one could not see through it to the grain of the wood underneath. Here and there I saw finger marks, clean islets in the midst of the gray. "It's so dirty in here and I have no time anymore to clean up. No time to clean myself, my house, my children. But I'm way beyond feeling ashamed and making excuses for the way everything looks. People just have to find pride in other ways. Maybe I could keep everything in order and looking pretty if I still had him around, but I don't . . ."

She motioned me to sit in the small upholstered armchair that blocked most of the passageway between the living room and small dining area, while she slumped down on a worn couch across the room. She lay her head back, stretched her feet out, straightened her skirt, and closed her eyes. I saw the perspiration collecting under her chin and around her neck.

"I'm not sleeping, just resting. So terribly tired all the time now. Working every day except Sundays, doing my church work on Sundays, it makes me very, very tired. Way down in my bones I can feel the tiredness creeping up. Starts in your bones and makes its way up in the tissues. Even my old skin seems tired. Tuesday, eh? Tuesday and four more days to come and go. I have all my children running around in the world this day, and I'm sitting here tired." She let her body relax while I made certain to look away. When she opened her eyes she would see me alert but politely looking elsewhere about the room. She would not know my own fatigue; nor would she think that my avoiding her eyes meant that I was inspecting her home.

"You're looking at my living room?" I heard her ask.

"No, just thinking, really, Mrs. Keller."

"Me too. I'm thinking too," she said.

"Would you be willing to share your thoughts?"

"I would, yes. I would. I want to make sure I'm not around when you speak with Adrien, or the others. I don't want my opinions to influence theirs, if you know what I mean." I nodded. "I'm sure they get a lot of their ideas from school, and from their mother. Now is when I think how much they might have used their father. You've been

asking these children about politics, eh? I imagine you want
to know who they like and what sorts of attitudes they have.
Isn't that it?"

"That's right, yes."

"Well now, you see those are the sorts of things that a family needs a father for. You take the elections. A person is
best to study up on the men who will be running; listen real
hard to what they have to say. Listen to their ideas and
more than anything, I suppose, what their promises for this
year might be. That's the important thing to be listening
for."

She was nodding her head as if agreeing with herself. I
saw her glance at the photograph, then quickly at me to see
whether I had noticed her. Then she smiled kindly. "You
realize that you and I must be almost the same age? I'm a
little bit older maybe, I would say. That's one of your differences in society, that we should be the same age and that
you should have such small children and that I should have
such grown-up children." I was missing a connection between the points of her argument and she saw my confusion.
"I'm leading up to my idea," she explained quickly. "I'm
leading up to the idea, don't you see, that the differences between poor folks and almost everybody else are found everywhere you look. You all wait before having children; we
have 'em right away. Maybe we don't think we can ever
have anything more important so we have 'em soon as we get
married. Sometimes we just have 'em and forget marriage, *and*
schooling, for that matter. You folks don't do that. You got
your ways though." She grinned.

"Now, what I was leading up to before is that we don't wait
because we know our history. We know our politics too."
Her look seemed authoritative. "We know exactly what is
coming to us, and most especially what is never *ever* going to

be coming to us." There was bitterness in her voice as she spoke to me not only as the representative of powerful people, but as a representative of the man in the White House himself. "They've been talking about programs for this and programs for that for years now. Ever since I was a kid, younger, way younger than Adrien, I've heard those promises. Jobs, day-care centers, housing, prices, wages. First my mother was telling them to me, explaining to all her children what politics was all about. Then it was the radio, sitting there, you know, with everybody crouched around, listening to the folks running for President. Now it's the television. Seeing 'em, all those powerful folks getting up in front of us, you, me, everybody, and making their same old promises." She lay back on the couch again and closed her eyes. She was shaking her head ever so slightly and raising her eyebrows at the same time. "Promises, promises, promises," she sighed. "Oh my sweet God, what I could own if every store would just let me pay them with promises." Her eyes opened wide and fixed directly on me. "So you don't ever have to remind me of promises, not when you've seen what I've seen and heard what I've heard, all my life. You never need to remind me. If there's reminding to be done around here, I guess I'll be the one to be doing it."

We sat in silence. She kept nodding yes, and I dared not interrupt her. I saw the void in this room, in this home, and in the lives of these five people left by the death of her husband, and by the ways society defines death and inheritance. Some people, surely, fill that void as if it were a cavern with drink or drugs. Mrs. Keller filled hers with work, and no doubt too with pledges to protect her children as best she could.

"When I was a child," I heard her say, "there was this enormous fire in the house across the street from where I lived. Oh, the firemen were coming from every which way, and the sirens were going off real loud, you know. I remember all the children — there were eight in my family besides my daddy and mamma — children from all the homes went outside to watch the firemen and all the trucks. Mamma thought we should stay in. 'We have no right,' she said, 'just to watch other people's tragedies forming.' But we went anyway, most of us, I think. We were only children, see. It was very exciting too. I remember the flames were flying up not so far from where we were standing. I remember how close we were because the police had to keep pushing us back. But we stayed there, must have been two hours easy. We'd get close and the police would have to push us back. My littlest brother got lost, I remember, by the time we finally went inside. Everybody got so scared, you know. It was the first time that night that we really got scared. We thought maybe he might have wandered near the fire and got himself killed or something. Know where he was?"

"No."

"In my mamma's bed fast asleep all the time. No one saw him go in there. He just got tired, so he went to bed."

I laughed. "Children," I said in the way that bespeaks their charm and unpredictability.

"Anyway, the next day, and the reason I'm telling you my recollections, we heard that six people died in the fire, each of 'em little children, just like we were. I remember I was so scared when I heard about it. Nothing bothered me the night before watching the fire, but when I heard about those children I thought I would faint right out, dead away on the floor like that." She stroked the air with her hand. "And my sister, the one who's a year older than me, when she heard the news she just all of a sudden threw up. All over herself too. Can you imagine? I don't like to confess it, but in bed that night, the night of the fire, you know, we were excited as you could possibly be about anything. We were lying in our bed upstairs there giggling and having ourselves one plain old fine time. We were even cursing that you couldn't see nothing of the fire out our window. The room didn't face out on the street, you see. And then, that next day my sister Eloise goes and throws up."

Now it was I shaking my head.

"Well, that was a serious business, something I never forgot, as you can see." She smiled faintly. Her eyes hunted in the room for the next thought. "I've got two things to tell you about that fire, two memories that I can see very, very plainly whenever I tell anyone that story. The first is that not until the next day when I heard the news about the six children dying did I think about the firemen and how hard they were working. I didn't think about any of the danger they might have been in. We were just having a good time, like I was telling you. But then, when I heard about those poor, poor little children, caught in all that smoke and heat, I thought about the firemen going into that house, risking their lives to save even one person and maybe not save any of them.

"Now, none of those firemen, that I remembered anyway, was a black man. There were only white men. Some young, some old. They knew they had to go into this building to help black folks. They knew it right from the get-go. No one white living anywhere in those blocks where we lived. Everybody black, the ghetto, like they say, although no one called it that. They called it Brownsville in those days." Her words were said with no apparent emotion. "But they went into that building all the same. Maybe they got hurt, no one ever said anything about firemen getting hurt that night, but they came, all of them, and they did what they

knew they had to do. They did their job, you might say."
She leaned toward me, resting her elbows on her knees.

"Now I know that those men did not like black folks. We
used to hear them talking from time to time when I was
growing up. We heard 'em in restaurants and around in
places where we went, you know. We were niggers to them.
Just nigger people. Not really people. We were black and
they were white and maybe in a fight they might have been
ready to kill us. Probably they would have too. But that
night they were doing their job. Whatever was in their
heart, it didn't make the slightest difference to them. That's
very important, don't you see." She paused, examining the
palms of her hands.

"Here's the second memory. The people who owned that
building — and now I'm telling you things I found out
much later 'cause we talked about that fire in my family over
and over again — got all kinds of insurance money paid to
them. I know that for a fact. They got *all* their money back
from that property. Fact is, I heard a story once, of course it
may not be true, that the man who owned that building
paid some black child to set it on fire." I moved in my
chair. "That's right," she repeated. "Paid him to *set* it on
fire for him. Now the child, this little boy, this is what I
heard, was a cousin of the children who lived and died in
that house. The man must have told him nobody would be
hurt because the fire would take so much time getting
started that everybody would be able to get out in time — "

"It's hard to believe," I interrupted.

"Well, like I say, it's only what I *heard*." She shrugged.
"Ain't no one going to be able to prove it one way or the
other." Her body relaxed and she leaned back on the couch.

"How old was the boy?" I was rubbing the side of my
face.

"Twelve."

"Twelve?"

"That's what I heard. Something like that. Twelve. Like my own Adrien."

"That's really something," I said.

"Sure, it is hard to believe. No sensible person wants to hear a thing like that, but it may not be so much when you think what one hundred dollars might mean to a little boy who's got to take care of a sick mother, an invalid and all, and of course her children too. Hundred dollars might take that family through a couple of months. The cold months even."

"But his own family."

"Don't you go looking so surprised," she said. "When you're desperate you have to take from your own. Who you going to be taking from anyway? Where do you think people are going to get money who can't get enough?" Even if she had been waiting for an answer, I could not have replied.

"Now here's where the politicians come into my story. You see, while that landlord got his money, the city promised to get some aid to that mother and father who lived across the street. Another family, we heard, took them in somewhere. It probably meant they had fifteen people in four rooms instead of only ten, but someone, you can be sure, took them in. But where was the money from the city?" She held her hands out in front of her. Her voice for this one sentence sounded plaintive and childlike. "Where was the money from the city that was promised to them?" This time she whispered the words. "It never came. The promises came." Her eyes were alive now, and perspiration flowed on her face. "They came all right, you can bet your shirt on that. But the money never followed."

Her look during the silence that followed said, That's my story. Do I have to say more? I watched her stand up and brush away some dust from the top of the dark brown table near the sofa. Wet with perspiration, Mrs. Keller inspected the dirt on her fingers before cleaning them on her dress. "See now what I mean by political promises? The firemen might hate the idea that they have to touch those black children, carrying them down the ladders and whatnot like they did. I'm not saying that they do, only that they *might*. But they risk their lives. No words about it, they just do their jobs. The politicians? Well, they got a whole wagonload of promises for poor folks. They even come around, have a drink of beer every once in a while, and it sure doesn't look to me like they got any hesitation about kissing our children, even the ones who come running into my house all dirty after school. Like my own Arthur. But ask them to lift their finger for you, ask them to give you the little money you might have coming from an insurance policy, and they look at you as if you were standing there half-crazy asking for a million dollars."

She ran her fingers along the side of her jaw feeling for the bone. Her eyes were clear, her posture erect and proud. Her whole appearance was more formidable than before. The discussions that followed her husband's death some five years ago had returned, and she was at last giving the speech she had never made.

"Just what kind of a political system are they running here anyway? Just what the hell kind of machinery do we have to put up with? Why won't somebody tell me that? Where's my tax money going every year? I'm busting my ass the same way as my husband did, the same way as my mother and father, and his mother and father too, and what have we got to show for it? Where's that crummy little bit of money I've got coming to me? It's all legal. Everything about it's legal. So why do they take it out of our paychecks if they aren't going to give it back when it's *coming* to us?" I thought she might have been crying but she was not.

"You don't hear me saying the government shouldn't get my money. You don't hear me complaining *once* about corruption and graft. What about all these big shots giving the plush jobs up there to their friends, and their family too. People don't even need those jobs except that their mothers and fathers are embarrassed 'cause their kids aren't working in the proper way. Why don't they give those jobs to *my* children? They haven't got a father anymore and I'm not ever going to bring them home another one. So why don't they help us, just for once, instead of putting the money into the pockets of people who've got 'em full already? They can't even fit it into one pocket, they got so much. They've got to get themselves bank accounts to hold all they got. I just about get it and I'm already spending it. So where's mine? Where's money for my children? I've got a boy who knew what to do with money when he was four years old, except I never had any to give him. So now they have a great political system, do they? All these rules about what you're supposed to do to get what ought to be yours all along.

"I'll tell you one more thing which I pray you'll see fit to put in that book you say you're going to write." She pointed her finger at me. Yes, ma'am, is what I wanted to say. "You see that picture of my husband?" I nodded yes, afraid to wipe my face dry for fear she would think I wasn't listening to her. "You know that when they come to inspect these buildings to see whether the city should fix 'em up, I hide that picture?" She saw my confusion. "Yessir. I put it away. Over there in that closet underneath my sheets and towels. That's where it goes. And do you know why?"

"I do not."

"Well, I'll tell you why. Because if those inspectors see that photograph they might be getting the wrong idea about me. They might think I have a husband who's run out somewhere to hide while they're doing all their little nosing around. You want to know about the politics they play around here? They don't always believe us when we say we *once* were married but now we lost our husbands. They don't believe us. Black women losing their husbands? They'd laugh in our faces. *Lose* your husband, honey, they'd say. You didn't *lose* him. He's just run out somewhere drunk, or chasing some woman so that you can get your welfare check! Poor folks, don't you see, they don't have their husbands *dying* on 'em. They either throw 'em out of their houses or hide 'em when the inspector persons come nosing around.

"Well, I don't need to take their welfare money. I work for mine. I work for every cent of it, and if they have to my children will be willing to do the same. But they're not going to work one minute, I'll tell you, if it means they have to miss one day of school. As long as I can walk they're going to work in that school and *make* it." She was almost breathless. "You'll see," she whispered, smoothing out her clothes that had wrinkled in the damp heat. "You'll see. It will be different someday." Her words were barely audible. She was about to speak again when we heard the sounds of children climbing the stairs outside in the hall.

"Day you beat me to the top, Robert, is the day you're smarter than me" are the words we heard. They preceded a series of thunderous explosions. The noise grew louder but ended when someone slammed against the front door. We could hear a boy breathing heavily. I looked at Mrs. Keller, who was waiting for someone to crash through the door.

Any minute, surely, the door would burst into a million pieces and there would be a child, utterly exhausted and hot but beaming with pride for having won a formidable race. Mrs. Keller turned to look at me, an expression of amusement on her face. She, too, wanted to know who won. We were rooting for the same boy.

"My sermon's over anyway," she said to me quietly. "You'll hear the rest another day. The wounds are still there." I said nothing. "Let's see who won," she suggested, walking to the door and opening it.

Ten-year-old Arthur Keller practically fell into the room. "Hey, what are you doing?" he cried out angrily before realizing it was his mother who had caused him to topple over. Seeing her he grinned sheepishly. Then, with more than a bit of pride, he proclaimed: "I won easily."

"Hell you did. You pushed me back there," his defeated school friend complained. "I'd have won easily."

"You're too fat," Arthur told him. "You can't ever beat me."

"Both of you shut your mouths and go get milk and cookies," Mrs. Keller ordered. "Get yourselves cooled off in there." She waited for them to move. "Go on, Arthur. Take your friend into the kitchen. Go on. You know Tom?"

"Yeah," the boy said shyly, passing by me.

"Now who's your friend here?" Mrs. Keller asked him.

"That's Robert. *You* know. He comes here all the time." I looked at Mrs. Keller. She seemed sad.

"Go on now and wash, please, before you eat," she told them. "And don't go messing up the kitchen so much that Adrien can't find her things for dinner." They were already out of sight. We heard them banging around in the kitchen, talking about the race and the heat in the apartment.

"Is that Robert Thurmond? Elice Thurmond's little boy?"

"I don't know," I answered. "I'm sorry."

"I'm home so little," she sighed. "The boy's right. I don't know his friends. I should."

I tried to shrug off her comment. "It's not so serious."

"It is," she replied forcefully. "It's as serious as anything I know. But the choice isn't mine." Glancing one last time in the direction of the kitchen, she reached for her purse and prepared to leave. I would wait for Adrien, Mrs. Keller would head downtown for the restaurant. She would arrive home that night somewhere between nine-thirty and ten. Quintin and Adrien would be awake. Arthur and a younger sister, Claudia, would be asleep. This was Tuesday afternoon. She would see them next on Thursday evening.

"Every minute I'm running," she said. "And when I'm not, I cry about my life to you. I'm going to take me a vacation someday if it's the last thing I do."

"I hope so," I said, reaching to get the door for her.

"You know it's hot in here." She smiled, leaving the room.

"Indeed I do," I said, at last wiping my face.

Within seconds she was at the top of the stairs. I closed the door but heard her stop outside. We had not said good-bye or arranged to meet again. Then I heard her turn around and knock on the door. I quickly opened it for her. Without entering the room, her room, she put her hand on my arm.

"Two things," she said. "One is that we didn't say good-bye. So good-bye to you."

"Good-bye, Mrs. Keller. I'll see you in a week or so."

"Good. I hope so," she said. "And two, the children shouldn't get overheated today. Make sure Adrien has a glass of milk. If we don't have any, buy her some. Here, I've got some change right here." She began hunting through her purse.

"Please, Mrs. Keller, let me. I'd like to." We were staring at one another, both of us thinking how complex was this one small act of buying milk. I could see her weighing the decision as though it were crucial that she make the right choice.

"I like you, Tom Cottle," she said. "I like the fact that you care about my children."

"That's good enough for me." My body relaxed and I smiled.

"But I'm not about to have you buying them what's my place to be buying them. So you give Adrien this money and tell her she should buy what she needs to fix dinner to-night and breakfast tomorrow, if anybody can eat with this weather." She handed me two dollars, smiled up at me, turned, and headed for the stairs.

Chapter 6

NOTHING ABOUT the culture of politics could seem more succinct than one's decision on whom to vote for. That pulling one lever mechanically precludes pulling the other lever testifies to the fact that on voting day most all political complexities are reduced to simple binary choices. Voting, therefore, appeals to the childlike part of me since complexity and compromise dissolve, and I am forced to choose either this or that.

Adrien and William D., too, experience this urge to reduce political realities to simple choice and easy explanations. Their day-to-day experiences, however, rule out such action. As much as they might wish to linger on simple yes or no questions, the teachings of their parents and their very own histories and perceptions reveal for them the forces that play upon them and keep them where they are in this city. Children are not only little people, they are shadow people whose needs and personalities are only indirectly faced up to. For their barest outlines to be visible, one needs the light of institutions and government to beat down on their bodies. But until children are granted rights, they remain shadows, and the rest of us need never confront them.

On a few occasions I spoke to William D. and Adrien about these matters of children's rights and the comprehensive need to abolish poverty. One might suspect, as I did, that they would seize these issues as their very own. Surely Adrien's shopping routines in the local Greenough Food Mart would make her sympathetic to any proposal or action that would ease the financial burdens of her family. But both children pushed aside my words — though not because they sounded outlandish. On the contrary: they sounded too much like luxuries that the children, ironically, feared.

Adrien and William D. are not inured to their circumstances, nor do they depend on these circumstances for their personal evolution. Their knowledge indicates that they have transposed gossip, classroom discussions, newspaper and television reports, and conversations into attitudes and even political stances on certain issues. But rarely in speaking to me do they appeal to their background or history. They size up the political fortunes and misfortunes of their people, keep their eyes and ears open, gather their information, make their calculations. Then they reestablish for themselves the complexities of politics, and remind me of the connections between abstract, depersonalized political theory and the content of the mind. They fear the punishment, lack of protection, abandonment, mistreatment they and their families have always experienced. To speak of change in the society is to arouse in them the experiences of hurt and death that regularly accompanied any attempt at change or personal and family improvement they have ever known about. It is not necessarily that they are cynical; they are doubtful, intelligently self-protective, knowledgeable of the histories of their parents, grandparents, and often great-grandparents as well, and concerned about the welfare of all these people. Openly hating those who would hurt them or steal from them is not easily managed. For if there is one thing worse than living their life as a shadow, they have told me in so many ways, it is to see even the shadow disappear.

Once, in a conversation with Adrien, I happened to mention a young man who works in the stock room of the Greenough Food Mart where she shops. "Anthony Driver," I announced his name, "from the track team."

"Yeah, that's right, you know him," she replied. Adrien remembered a conversation she, Anthony, and I had had less than a year before about food prices. Anthony, a seventeen-year-old high school student, had told us that a group of young people were planning measures to force food-store owners to reduce prices. Realizing that prices were not only increasing but were already higher at the Mart than at a dozen stores they had surveyed in nearby communities, they tried to organize a boycott. The idea frightened Adrien. She feared that when the authorities discovered the plans for a boycott, they would punish the entire community and raise food prices across the board.

"You'll see," she said. "The police are going to come down hard on all those people and the rest of us ain't going to have anything to eat after that. We'll be eating cereal boxes by the time they get through."

"But they're so high already," I argued. "You yourself say they're going up and up."

"You'll see. You'll see what they'll do. They're going to starve us. We're going to come in here one of these days and there's going to be no food anywhere. First they'll raise the prices we can't afford milk anymore, and then when they know we're staying at home dying of hunger, they'll take the rest of the food away."

"It won't happen." But I was unable to console her. The thought of rising food prices and going hungry to the point of death overwhelmed her and she became frantic. She was angry and despairing, wanting to hit out at anyone she saw.

"You'll see," she screamed as I walked her home, barely

able to keep up with her furious pace. "They can take stuff out of there any time they want to. They got these trucks that pull up to the back of the store. They'll load them up with all the canned goods and bottles and boxes, everything, and leave all the stuff that dies for us. Then they'll throw open those big doors they got there in the front and we'll go rushing in some morning like usual thinking everything's just like it always is, and then we'll be loaded down with dead fish and rotten eggs and smelly milk. Worms in the stuff too, and molds on the bread."

"Adrien, come on. You're blowing this thing way out of proportion. All Anthony and his friends are planning is a boycott. They work. Often they work to get the prices down." I told her about a milk boycott several years before that had proceeded as smoothly as any protest could. Within three days the dairy that had raised the prices and the large supermarket that stocked the dairy's products capitulated and the prices were lowered to their previous levels. "It couldn't have been easier. No one got hurt; no one starved," I said. "In fact, there were some very important people involved in that boycott and no one was about to mess with them." She apparently did not hear a word.

"We're going to starve," she said, starting to cry. "The police will come in before it's all over and we'll be poisoned. You can't tell whether what you put in your mouth is any good. Nobody can tell. How do you know? How you going to be able to tell? You don't know. I hear all the time how they got lousy food they put in our stores. They know it's no good but they put it there all the same. No one cares if *we* get it. They just figure no one's ever going to know why we got so sick."

"Adrien," I pleaded with her. The talk with Anthony Driver had detonated something inside of her.

"You told me yourself." She turned and pointed her finger at me. "You said that stores where you live don't carry that bad paint we get here. *You* were the one who told me and my mother that day how your friend in the hardware store, you remember, wouldn't let you buy that orange paint you saw 'cause he was afraid your little girl might get some of it in her mouth someday? *You* told me that! Remember?"

"I do," I said quietly. "The lead in the paint. I remember. But it's different with that stuff, Adrien. It really is."

"Hell it is," she cried. "You're lying to me right now, because you told my mother and me how you talked to the hardware man around our house and how they had the same paint that could kill us and they weren't about to change it. You can't be telling me no different. I *know* people who've been killed by that stuff, so don't go telling me different."

When we reached her home, Mrs. Keller, who was on her way out, met us at the top of the stairs. "Well now, what's got into you, girl, crying like that?" she asked.

"Nothing," Adrien replied bitterly, marching right past her into the house. Mrs. Keller looked quizzically at me. "What in the name of the Lord were you two talking about today?" There was exasperation in her voice.

"Adrien, I think, got frightened," I began my explanation, "by some guys who were — "

"Were *what?*" she interrupted anxiously.

"Not *that,* Mrs. Keller. They were talking about plans for a boycott at the Greenough Food Mart sometime soon because over the last six months the prices have gone so high, and apparently they're going even higher."

"That's all? Thank God it was only that."

"That's all it was. It frightened Adrien because she suddenly got it into her head that when the authorities hear about the boycott they might starve or poison the people." I gave Mrs. Keller a look: children and their runaway fantasies. But her serious expression remained unchanged.

"And you think," she replied firmly, "that it couldn't happen, I suppose? You think that these children get these notions about starving, or maybe being poisoned, out of the thin air, do you?"

"No, I don't at all." Don't use me as any straw man, Mrs. Keller, is what I wanted to say to her. But like an obedient child, I stood there on the landing waiting for her permission to speak.

"Well, I would hope not, because you know there's not a child in this world really makes up things that scare them. Everything they are afraid of is something they've really seen or heard. You never know what, exactly, but they've seen them. Monsters, dragons, whatever it is they dream about — and I can tell you that some of their dreams are mighty strange 'cause I'm the one who has to get up with them in the middle of the night — all those things are things they've seen, or *believed* they saw. So when my little girl tells you that folks may not get enough food, or that they're going to be poisoned, then you can be damned sure she got that idea from someone somewhere.

"I don't know, you see, what *your* children go dreaming, but *my* children know *all* about poverty: the dying, the hunger, the illness. That's what's in their dreams. Real things, real problems are what they have running around in their heads. Ain't no telling how and when those things are going to be coming back out, but that's real stuff they fear. I can tell you that. They got politics in their dreams. Food prices, civil rights, wars, losing people out of their families when they aren't ready for it, all different varieties of mistreatment, their schools, all of it goes into their heads and nothing, but nothing, comes out again in the same way. They just hold it there 'til something on the outside scares them, like the boy must have done just now. Then it comes out. It's like a cat jumping off a window. There she sits" — Mrs. Keller pointed beyond the stairs leading to the next floor at an imaginary window — "waiting, waiting, waiting. All day long she may sit up there, not doing anything, just looking around, taking in the world, you get what I mean? To look at her you'd think she was sleeping; got these heavy eyes she blinks real slowly. But she's taking in every little thing she sees and putting it away in her mind. Then all of a sudden, if you scare her or push her the wrong way, she ups and jumps, and that's it. Bang!

"That's the way it is with all God's children. They take in everything and no one can say for sure when they'll jump down from where they were setting. Just like that cat." She motioned again toward the stairs. "But the children around here are different, I suspect, from the children you see most of the time. They're just a little different from them. Children here got poverty surrounding them everywhere they go. Anyplace they go they see poverty. Even those times when you take Adrien and the Williams child . . ."

"William D.," I reminded her.

"Yes, William D. When you take them someplace near your school over there in Cambridge, or downtown, they still see poverty. They see rich places with their eyes, but they see their own homes with their hearts. And that's something there isn't a politician in the world, as far as I'm concerned, can ever understand. 'Cause even the good ones who come from places just like this, homes just like this one, they've forgotten how you're supposed to see with your heart. They got their eyes working all right, but their hearts stopped seeing a long, long time ago. Heaven only knows what kind of dreams they have. Probably they don't dream anymore. They forget what hunger's all about. They may say they don't forget but it sure seems to me like they do. When they come into these communities and tell us all the time how they remember, then I say to myself, they don't remember anything. If they did, they wouldn't have to remind everybody about it. All they'd have to do is look at these places and cry with us." She was almost whispering.

"Delicate the way children's minds work. Any minute something just comes flying out. Like that cat up there, ready to spring. Those are the things you have to know if you want to know about children — not all those things they say when they're just talking to you real sober, but what they're dreaming about in the night.

"Okay, that's enough of that." Her tone changed. "Now, I want you to go inside my home, and find that child of mine and talk with her some more. Go in to one of your kitchen meetings. Tell her things are pretty hard but that we haven't hit the bottom just yet." Mrs. Keller had already begun to descend the stairs. Her simple movement seemed to involve great effort. "We may be getting close, and come November we may be even closer than we are right now, but we haven't hit the bottom yet." She had reached the landing between the floors when I heard her say, "Though God knows there are mornings when I get out of bed and sure do believe I can see it before my eyes."

The sense of seeing the bottom was something that Adrien too had often felt. It was increased by the inventory of possessions she took periodically, sometimes unwittingly. Seeing the bottom was not merely a symbolic suggestion. It meant finding empty cupboards and empty spaces in the trays of the refrigerator. It meant the feeling of loss and of not getting what should be coming to you, what others seem to have in abundance, and of having objects taken away and never replaced. At the moment of feeling these deprivations, of seeing that bottom, she and her brothers and sisters turned by necessity and with hope to their mother, as though her words might fill this newly felt emptiness.

The Kellers had in fact been robbed during the past summer. It was the third time in less than two years. A radio had been taken from the kitchen, which angered Adrien since it was her special work companion, along with several pieces of jewelry. They included two of her mother's necklaces, several small brooches, and her father's wrist watch.

"Nothing of great value," her mother informed me right after the robbery, "just stuff that matters more than money because it all lay against the bodies of your loved ones. I had this brooch that rested every day, morning and night, on the bosom of my mother. Man that took that will be lucky to get five dollars for it, but I wouldn't have sold it for ten million dollars."

"Ten million dollars?" Arthur repeated wide-eyed.

Mrs. Keller looked past her son at me. "You see how these children are? All they could care about is what things cost. Everything always has to be big money. That's right, Arthur" — she turned to him — "I wouldn't have sold those brooches that your grandmother wore every day of her life for ten million dollars!"

"You're crazy, Mom," Arthur said scratching his ear, turning on a heel, and leaving us alone with Adrien. "Ten million dollars," he muttered as he reached the kitchen. The rest of us smiled.

"You can understand my feeling for that jewelry, can't

you, Adrien?" Mrs. Keller asked her daughter. Adrien merely nodded. "Course you can. Men, boys, they can't understand what all these little trinkets might mean to a woman."

"I think Arthur could understand, like, about Daddy's watch," Adrien said quietly.

"Yes, I suppose he can understand that," her mother agreed. "I suppose he can. But I can understand, too, why that boy would want money. I guess I want it too. We all do." The thought reminded her of the robbery, and her body suddenly lurched with anger. "Nerve of that man coming into this house and robbing us like that. What do people like him expect to find when they come into houses like ours? You'd think a man who's dumb enough to suspect we have something after looking at the outside of this house and at the stairwell out there just *has* to get caught. Police ought to have him in a minute."

"Won't they catch him?" Adrien wanted to know.

"Never." Mrs. Keller sounded emphatic. "No one will ever see him again. He's gone for good. He'll fence our stuff and hit someone else tomorrow, maybe the next day. They won't catch him. There's too many of his kind going around getting away with whatever they want. Robbing decent people and all."

"It isn't fair," Adrien protested. I rarely heard her sound so frustrated. "Why'd they have to pick on us again?"

"Take it easy now, Adrien. You got to understand that these things happen." Mrs. Keller had calmed down. To me she said, "Child her age doesn't understand the way all this robbery stuff works. Why do you think, girl," she inquired of her daughter, "they go robbing people's homes in the first place?"

"You mean like ours?" Adrien wanted to know.

"Anybody's home," Mrs. Keller replied rather gruffly. "Why do men steal? Why do you think they take these little things that mean so much to people like ourselves?"

" 'Cause they want money," her daughter answered obediently.

"That's right. And just why do you suppose they need all that money?"

" 'Cause they take drugs and they drink all the time."

"You think so, eh?" Mrs. Keller responded. "Everybody thinks that, I guess." She sounded not unlike a sociologist lamenting the fact that common prejudices too often substitute for the truth. "Well, sir," she said regarding the two of us, "Tom here knows that isn't the case, don't you, Tom?" I made an ambiguous gesture. I wanted to communicate to Mrs. Keller that I knew better than to think that all stolen money goes to purchase drugs, and yet at the same time tell Adrien that my first response to her mother's question resembled her own. "No, daughter, it's because they can't find jobs nowhere. Give the man that took my mamma's brooch a good clean, honest job that he can call his living, and a roof over his head, and you won't find him in anybody's home but his own. I guarantee you that."

"And what about the drugs?" Adrien asked bitterly. Her anger was exacerbated by her mother's seeming compassion for the thief and her somewhat pedantic manner.

"Drugs? Well, some people surely need their habit kept up," Mrs. Keller conceded. "But all this robbing that's going on in this city can't for a single minute be due to *just* the drug trade."

"So why do they rob *us?* We haven't got drugs in here." Adrien asked.

For an instant, Arthur poked his head back into the living room to listen to his mother.

"Go 'way, boy. This isn't for your ears," Mrs. Keller

shouted to him. Then to Adrien: "Course we don't, child. Course there aren't drugs around here. But that man, he doesn't expect drugs to be lying around in here. He sees children playing around in here, so he knows there are parents somewhere about, or at least one older person." She looked at me. Adrien caught the look. "So he figures: parents, money, robbery. Just like that. He's not looking for drugs, 'cause he can't find anything like that here." I smiled at her, and despite the intensely positive feelings I hold for this woman, I confess at that moment to wondering whether I would know it if Mrs. Keller used drugs.

"But why us, Mamma?" Adrien persisted.

"Because, child, the poor got to rob each other! There's no one else for them *to* rob. The ghetto, where we live, is like one big prison. When we travel from city to city, anywhere in the world even, all we're doing is changing from one prison to another. So when we get robbed, all it is is one prisoner robbing from another, just like in real prisons."

"So why don't they rob rich folks?" Adrien asked.

Mrs. Keller smiled. She began to nod her head up and down as though she had anticipated this very question. "Because if you want to go and rob rich folks, you got to get out of prison first. The rich keep us in here and make us rob each other. You read in the papers from time to time about some rich man getting robbed in his home, or on a street near where he lives maybe. But you don't see reporters coming down here to these parts just to write a story about *us* getting robbed. Only time we make a good story for them is when we get all hot and bothered and go lighting up the city protesting some law or new decision they've made. We're *just* like prisoners. Crime? They couldn't care less about crime, unless, of course, it's one of their own. In that way they're just like us."

Adrien didn't move a muscle. Balancing herself on the

arm of her mother's chair, she listened to the words, imagining things, no doubt, tucking away ideas for later on.

"Crime in the streets," her mother concluded, "and law and order sure are nice slogans for those politicians. But around here there isn't a living soul who believes anyone has his eye on helping us. All they think about is that people from here are going to make their way into the suburbs and take where the taking is real good. This here's a case for you, Tom Cottle. We got poor folks so tied up in this country, so locked in tight in their prisons, we don't even let 'em rob where the robbing is good. It's like the man used to say, If you're going to pick apples, no sense you standing around the bushes. You better get yourself over to the biggest tree."

If Adrien was understandably preoccupied with robbery, then William D. examined the crime issue in terms of murder and untold violence. Although he had never presented me with a list of significant political causes, murder and police work were especially important concerns to him.

One afternoon before the elections, we spoke for several hours about the police in his community. Prompted possibly by talk of law and order and the speculations of who might be Boston's new police commissioner, the topics of police and crime were ones William D. had been eager to pursue. He stood against the doorway of his home, one leg crossed over the other. I was about to descend the stairs. Mention of the word "police," however, caused him to stand up to attention and he asked me to stay a few more minutes.

"We haven't talked enough about the police and crime. That's politics too, ain't it?" he asked as I quickly climbed the few stairs and stood alongside him on the landing. He unlatched the front door and quietly pulled it closed. "This isn't for my mother," he said.

"The issue of crime in the streets, William D.?" I prodded
him.

"Yes, and no. There's a lot of killing around here, you
know. Every night when I'm lying in my bed I hear the sirens going outside. Sometimes they shoot up Bowdoin Street
but mostly they're out there heading down South Plaine.
Lots of police cars, all hours of the morning too. They used
to wake up my baby sister. I'd hear my mother or father getting up with her, bringing her into bed with them so's she
would shut up. Even when she was little" — he held his
hands up to measure a distance of less than a foot — "she
could yell loud enough to wake us all up." This he announced with pride.

"That little, eh?" I teased him.

"Hmm. She could get the whole neighborhood up if she
really wanted to." Whereas in the beginning he had seemed
eager to tell me of something, his manner now was dream-
like and wistful. For some people, I thought, crime means
being awakened by sirens as well as fearing that one might
be molested, burgled, raped, or murdered.

"You wanted to tell me something, William D."

"You got to go, man?"

"Well, no. I thought we had just about talked ourselves
out, though. Should I leave?"

"Well, I guess I don't have anything else. I was just thinking about crime, you know, and it being another thing for us
and politics."

"I think it may be more," I suggested.

"Why?"

" 'Cause you closed the door."

"Oh yeah." His manner seemed disingenuous.

"Tell me."

"What?"

"I don't know, William D. You tell me what, okay?"

He waited a moment, looking around at nothing in particular, then he spoke.

"I had this big dream I wanted to tell you. It's not true, it's only this dream, right?"

"Right."

"Well, like, in the dream, they say my father is supposed to have committed this serious crime. I never find out what it is really. I only know that he was supposed to have done it." By this time, we had sat down on the steps. Our bodies were touching but we were both staring straight ahead. "Then one morning the cops come to take my father away. I don't see them, but I hear them ordering him around. One of 'em sounded like one of my teachers, come to think of it. Mr. Henry. Real tough, you know. But my dad, he's there yelling back at 'em that he's innocent, that he didn't do whatever they said he did, you know. I hear him telling 'em he doesn't even know what they're talking about. But they just say that all criminals talk like that. Nobody ever does anything, they say. Everybody's always innocent.

"Anyway, he's begging them to let him go, but they keep telling him he's got to come downstairs — all of this was taking place here, inside the house — and get into the car with them, so they could take him in, you understand?"

"Right. And you're listening to all this?" We still hadn't looked at one another.

"Yeah. I'm hiding somewhere, like in a room next to where they are, except we don't have a room there. But it's all in the dream. So, I'm just there listening. Then all of a sudden I hear this explosion, bang, and I say to myself, Someone's shooting and I have to go out in the hall to see what's happening, except I'm afraid my dad might be, you know — "

"Killed or wounded," I interjected.

"Yeah, that's right. So I wait in the room and then I hear him say, 'And you're going to get it too.' Then there's another shot and this time I hear someone fall and I know my father's killed 'em both. Then he calls me, 'cause somehow he knows I'm hiding in this room, and he tells me I've got to help him. Then he opens this cabinet or closet there and inside he's got all these guns stacked up. Hundreds of 'em. Rifles. All of 'em are rifles. And he says, 'Take 'em; you know how to use 'em. Take 'em. We'll go over to the window and pick 'em off. Nobody's coming to get me. We'll be safe.' Then, you know how dreams are. Like, you suddenly know how to shoot a gun even though you really don't know how to. So I'm hiding below the window with my dad and we're shooting policemen, and getting 'em, all of 'em. Bang, bang, bang all over the place. Some of 'em are climbing up this big ladder like they were firemen, and we're just shooting 'em real easy. We never miss. It's like on television. None of 'em bleeds, although I didn't think about that until just now. But anyway, we're shooting, and every time I run out of bullets I just grab another gun. It's real loud, and weird too, because I'm firing away there even though, like I say, I don't know anything about guns."

"Does your dad, William D.?"

"About guns?"

"Yeah."

"No. I don't think so."

"Does he have a gun?"

"I never saw one. I don't think so." I watched him trying hard to recall any reference to his father carrying a gun. "In the army he shot a gun probably, but I never saw him there."

"I interrupted you. I'm sorry, go on."

"With the dream, you mean?" he asked.

"Yes."

"Well, here's the end of the dream. There's some other stuff, but I can't remember it good. Sometimes dreams are like movies, you can't remember parts of 'em. They sort of skip around.

"I remember that I wasn't scared at all. I just knew, like, that nothing was going to happen to us. The policemen kept coming up at the window and we kept shooting 'em and they kept falling. I never saw their faces. I remember thinking about their blue uniforms and their gold buttons, and that maybe I could keep some of their hats. Then I began to worry that maybe there was a way the police could get us from behind, but there were no doors in the room. I even thought about helicopters landing on the roof like they do on television. I think I was thinking about television in the dream, getting ideas from it, but I can't remember exactly. Anyway, I just knew, like before, that the only way they could get us was through this one window where we were really doing it to them. It didn't even bother me that I was killing them. It didn't feel like anything special or different. I was just there next to my father.

"Here's the end coming up now." William D. stretched his arms and legs as if he wanted to move to a different step. He glanced in my direction, then decided to stay where he was. "See, pretty soon I figured that we had this serious problem. My father wasn't thinking about it but I was."

"That you might get into trouble for killing cops?"

"No. Not that. Worse. See, the policemen were piling up outside. We were in our house, although it didn't look exactly like our house in the dream, but we were on the third floor. Like here. But the bodies were getting piled up higher and higher, and I figured that pretty soon if we just kept shooting like we were doing we wouldn't be able to shoot 'em 'cause we couldn't see 'em. They were like this big blue mountain." The fright he had experienced during the dream had returned. I felt him trembling as he urged himself to finish the account. "It was going to get real dark, I figured, but my father was there shooting away like before. I guess he didn't think about what I was thinking about.

"Then I thought of something else. If the bodies kept piling up higher and higher they would be in front of the window, you know, covering it up all the way around, and then we wouldn't have any air in the room, 'cause this was the only window, like I said. Then I really got scared, 'cause I figured either way we're going to die. Either we kill the cops and die 'cause we ain't got enough air, or we stop shooting 'em and let 'em come in and kill us in the room."

I was about to speak, to offer words of relief that this had only been a dream, when William D. added his final thought.

"All during the dream I had this funny feeling inside me that maybe the police were doing the right thing and that maybe I was doing the wrong thing, you know. Like, maybe my dad really *was* a criminal only he never told me anything about it. I was thinking that maybe I should have asked him before we started all this killing we were doing, but I didn't. He just said, 'C'mon and shoot,' so I did. I kept looking over at him all the time expecting that he was going to change into someone else, and not be my father at all, you know."

When he finished we sat on the steps, neither of us speaking for a long time.

The nature of government, employment conditions, social classes, laws, and rights, I thought, that exist within any community and outside it as well forever influence a child's development, intelligence, and sense of self. This means that bureaucratic inefficiency or overload on welfare rolls in one part of the culture affects a boy's sense of his relationship with his father in another part of the culture. It means too that orderly political protest against rising food prices causes terror in a girl to whom this dissent may have been originally dedicated. Racism and poverty, moreover, cause children with proven sophistication to doubt their families, and then to keep from themselves this doubt for fear of retribution.

If an aggregate of people, therefore, is deprived access to the fundamental rights, privileges, and spaces of their society, it may well cherish the specialness that its emerging "subgroup" and "subterrain" yield. But these deprivations will also shape the movement of people in space and supply, in their complex ways, the fixings of the imagination, even for children whose fantasies often seem to us anchored to nothing at all. All literature written about children, therefore, touches children, if only because it is incorporated by those out there, the politicians and nonpoliticians, whose impressions and attitudes ultimately determine the extent of any child's freedom.

"Some weird dream, man," William D. said, almost to himself.

"It must have been a frightening one," I replied.

"Know what I think? I used to think that dreams don't really mean anything. You know, that they were not really a part of you somehow. Just imaginary stuff. But now I don't think so. I think dreams are real, man. I really do. It's like your mind takes in everything you see and everything you hear and everything you're thinking about — even if you don't know you're thinking about it — and grinds it all up like in a big Mixmaster and spits it out, and that's a dream."

"I agree," I said quietly.

"But that means" — William D. began to stand up and

turn toward me as though to present a lecture — "that all these crimes that people commit every day make your mind start working. And all those sirens I hear, they go into my dreams too. Every time I hear about somebody being killed or robbed or something, that stuff can get into my mind too, and maybe in a dream someday. I mean some night."

"It's a great argument for law and order," I muttered under my breath.

"What did you say?" William D. wanted to know.

"I said" — more loudly this time — "that no one really knows the impact on our minds of crime, and people hurting one another, and people taking things from one another."

"Law and order is what you said though, right?"

"Right. Law and order," I repeated.

"That's an important political thing they're always talking about."

"It sure is," I sighed.

"Does it mean we get to be protected?" he wanted to know.

"I think it probably means more, William D. I think there's a certain controlling of people that's implied; making sure people behave. It puts certain limitations on political demonstrations and dissent." I had not been careful in my definition for him, but as I spoke I could already see him retreating to another thought.

"I think it's good," he said when I paused for breath.

"What's that?"

"Law and order. Because everyone's running around doing whatever they want and hurting people."

"But that's not exactly what is meant by law and order," I argued.

"Well, then, call it something else. They got to have something, don't they? I could be killed just like that. You could be killed just like that too." He snapped his fingers with each imaginary murder.

"And people can be wrongly accused," I added. He didn't see the connection of this thought to his dream. "Like in your dream with your father."

"Oh yeah. That could happen too. They could send the police right here to my home now and arrest me if they wanted to."

"But that might be a part of law and order too, William D."

"Well, it's okay," he decided after a moment of reflection. "If they think I did something, then they can come."

On this point we argued. Arresting people on suspicion, I tried to point out, could be seen as a threat to one's liberty. That was my line, along with the idea that people are innocent until proven guilty. William D. felt my argument to be foolish. "Protection" was the word he used again and again. Simple, everyday protection. His home had to be protected, his family too, and himself. "A person's never safe," he said repeatedly. "And something else. Here's what you're forgetting, Tom. If they stop all these crimes by sending the police around and arresting people who look suspicious and all, then children won't be so frightened. Like my baby sister, I mean."

"And she won't cry." I smiled.

"Right. And I won't have my weird dreams. If nobody's out there shooting up these places then I'll have nice thoughts for my mind to put into the Mixmaster. Remember, like I told you? Then I'll have all sorts of pretty dreams. No more killing in my dream. No more scary things." He scratched his head as though hunting for one last item for me. "No more politics in my dreams." He had a wide grin on his face and a generous, even hopeful look in his eyes.

Chapter 7

ON THE WEDNESDAY following the elections it rained in Boston. It was an angry rain that hit the city. Some laughingly proposed that the weather signified the President's revenge for having been defeated in Massachusetts.

Driving to the Williamses' home I thought about the candidates, now a winner and a loser, and how children in this and other communities often derogate politicians and speak of them in terms of "messing with" power and money. Many politicians seem corrupt, untouchable, and not quite human. Or perhaps they were once human, for the children hear it said that "he was a good man until he became mixed up with politics."

Paradoxically, my conversations with children reveal that politicians possess something superhuman, a potential to bring hope. Children glow with excitement watching a political parade and from being so close to that special man. They desire, perhaps, to be transported by this figure, or at least touched by him. And if he tells them that he grew up in a home like theirs and played in streets like theirs, then an alliance between them is established that carries the strength of religion as well as family. It is the seeing that is the believing. Just to see a candidate up close is enough to make these children believe that they themselves are people of worth.

Politicians, naturally, recognize their power, just as they recognize that parents and teachers are not always certain how to respond to this power in the presence of children. I have heard parents tell their children, "Don't you go believing that man, he's not out to help us." I have also watched parents hiding their cynicism and outrage so that the children may treasure their own reactions to a politician. "Yes, he is handsome, isn't he?" they will say. "It certainly would be nice to know him. Well, let us hope he can make all those things he says come true."

For such a rainy afternoon the scene in the Williams home seemed especially inviting and pleasant. Lamps were burning and Mrs. Williams had just finished straightening up the living room. Company was coming that evening. Several couples would be getting together to watch television, play some cards, maybe even talk a little politics.

"Tom Cottle's here," Mrs. Williams yelled down the short hall in the direction of the bedroom William D. shares with his brother. "He's all busy with something today," she explained to me. "Boy stayed up too late last night watching that stuff on television. His father told him that it was all settled and he should go to bed, but he insisted we let him watch. Can't talk with him when he gets it in his head to do something." She seemed miffed by something but I kept silent. "The elections made you sad, eh?" she asked rhetorically.

"Yeah, I guess they did."

"I suppose us too. You hate to see a man get beat so bad, not that we actually cared that much one way or another. We voted and all, but it never seems to matter too much around here. Maybe at your end of town it matters a little bit more. Your job isn't in trouble though, is it?" she asked suddenly.

"No, I don't think so. Unless of course you've heard something that I haven't," I joked.

"Now why should *I* hear anything about *your* job." She

was not smiling. "Some jobs, I heard today, may be in trouble 'cause of this. They said the man is going to pull back some of the money to the state."

"You mean because Massachusetts went for McGovern?" I asked.

"Nah." She seemed amused by this suggestion. "The man was going to cut out jobs here no matter what happened yesterday. He doesn't care that he lost here. He goes on and makes his plans just like before. He was probably making all kinds of decisions before he even found out what happened. He's not the kind of person who wants to get dirty with the people.

"William D.," she shouted down the hall again. "You hear me? Tom Cottle's waiting on you out here. Boy's spiteful as well as being deaf," she grumbled. Returning to her chores she asked again whether I was all "shook up" by the election results. I told her no, that I had been expecting it. Many people had been predicting it would be closer than it was, but they too were expecting the worst.

"The worst?" she reacted with bitter surprise. "That's what you call the worst? Four more years of Mr. Nixon? That ain't the worst. Lots of things could be far worse. Look around you. Look in this house, and in these streets. Now aren't they worse to you than four years of that man? Lots of things worse than him being in the White House. Dying is worse, fighting wars is worse, going hungry and tired every day is worse too. Not having enough money is worse. You haven't got it all that bad. You'll survive the next four years, we all will, if we just see fit to take care of ourselves. That's what we got to do."

"And you, Mrs. Williams?" I expected a complicated answer, but it was not forthcoming.

"We're going to survive too. We got to take care of ourselves too. That's all anybody can do now. You see, you had some little spark in you that said if only McGovern can just make it there will be all kinds of changes coming. But like I told you once, you remember, I'm older. I understand a little better what really happens in these elections. I know you understand more about politics 'cause you study it and all at the university, but I have other kinds of impressions." As she spoke she began to sweep the floor in the corner of the room farthest from where I sat. "The way I see it, these elections make very little difference. Very little difference ever. William D. and us were talking about this very thing last night after the television was finished. He doesn't really understand it. He thinks you change Presidents and the whole country is going to turn right around and be different. Everything's going to be all clean, you know, good places to look out for your children, and nobody's going to have any more problems. But what I've seen in the last years is that politics is a whole lot like families, and the man who is the President is a lot like a father in the family. The mother is, well, she's kind of like the country, changing a little, you know, getting bigger around the edges as she gets older, and maybe a little wiser too." Mrs. Williams laughed to herself as though her last image was particularly illicit. "Now all of this makes the people, all those folks going out there yesterday like you and my husband and me, the children in that family. Father, mother, and children is equal to the President, the country, and all the rest of us little children voting every four years."

"Which makes the cabinet the President's little brothers, who he gets to push around," I added.

"Yeah." She grinned. "That's part of it too, I suppose. He pushes 'em around all right too, doesn't he? Well now, where was I?"

"With the — "

"Yeah. I got it. Now, in this family, if you suddenly have a death, or a divorce, which is kind of what happens when they switch Presidents, except for President Kennedy, which was horrible. That was a death, you see, and everyone was shocked. That wasn't supposed to happen. God, God no. That was never supposed to be." She stood quietly, holding on to the broom handle with both hands, staring at the wall, and shaking her head. My own thoughts turned to the fact that to this day I cannot look at pictures of President Kennedy without the discomfort of ten years ago returning. "No," she was saying quietly, "President Kennedy, that was not in God's plan." She paused again before speaking. I heard William D. singing in his room. The door opened and he headed for the living room.

"Well," Mrs. Williams resumed, "the normal way they switch Presidents is more like a divorce or separation than a death. One man moves out, another man moves in. He brings in his stuff, you know, his belongings and his friends, and everybody just goes on like before. Things don't suddenly get any better having this new man around; they probably don't get any worse either. Everything stays just about the same. Families make things stay just about the way they were, I suppose, and governments do too. The country goes on."

"Like the mother," I interjected.

"Yeah. But the voters go on too."

"The children," we said in unison.

"The children," she repeated, "they just go on too. Sick or well, they go on."

"Who's sick?" William D. wanted to know, overhearing his mother's last words.

"Nobody's sick." She smiled at him. "Tom and me, we were just, well, making up some ideas."

"About what?" William D. asked.

"About you and politics," she answered quickly. Her words masked my own, "political theory."

"Sounds cool to me." William D. grinned at his mother. "She knows a lot," he said to me. "Dad talks a lot about politics, but she knows a lot too, don't you, Mom?"

Mrs. Williams appeared embarrassed but proud.

"Don't she, Tom?"

"She knows an awful lot, William D."

"I know what I know and nothing more," Mrs. Williams declared from her station in the corner. "I know that I got one helluva lot of work to do in this house before my company starts banging down that door tonight, which I now see, Tom Cottle, you didn't close tight when you came in."

"Oh my God." I rushed up out of my chair and ran to the door acting like a chastised old man. In my excitement and comedic way I purposely overplayed my penitence by bolting the door a second time. William D. laughed loudly while Mrs. Williams looked amused, though a trifle perplexed. She stood with her arms folded in front of her, embracing the light green broom handle. I gave her an exaggerated look of: What should I do now? I'll do anything to make up for my crime. She began to laugh, which only made William D. laugh harder.

"That the way you perform in front of your students?" she asked at last.

"Just about," I replied. William D. was clapping gaily.

"Well then," she said, "tell me this one, Professor. If you got the door locked so nice and tight like you do, from the inside, how you planning to let my husband inside when he comes home tonight from work, which he ought to be doing in less than two hours?"

I knew of course that I had made this mistake, but her

words allowed me to repeat my comedy antics with the door hardware.

"There he goes again," William D. shrieked.

"Man's crazy," I heard Mrs. Williams say. "You got a crazy man for a friend there, William D. I sure hope you can straighten him out before he leaves here tonight. Hate to find out what his old lady must think of him."

A bit of the tension between Mrs. Williams and me had eased. For a moment I had endeared myself to her, at least I had made her laugh. It is the age-old device, I thought, walking down the narrow hall with William D. to his bedroom. Jesters, comedians, both seek acceptance by becoming objects of humor, and for the duration of their performance the space between themselves and their audiences, like their own anxiety, is lessened.

William D.'s room could not have been more messy. Nothing looked to be in its place, if indeed anything ever had a place.

"It looks like a landslide hit this room."

"A what?" he shouted at me despite the fact that we were standing less than three feet from one another.

"A land — I mean a hurricane."

"You said a landslide." William D. poked his fist at my hip.

"That's what I said."

"Like last night's landslide, right?"

"Worse," I answered.

"Worse?" He pretended to be hurt. "You think this is worse in here than last night?"

"Much worse." I nodded imperiously. "Yessir."

"Why do you think it's worse?" he asked, his pride injured.

" 'Cause at least I can find a place to sit down in the United States, but in here you have to stand up all the time."

William D. giggled and began to throw his junk, school books, and clothes off the bed. I heard his mother yell something from the living room to him about cutting down the noise and "not to forget that people live downstairs too, even if you are thoughtless enough to forget about them." William D. shrugged his shoulders. He moved about the room making gestures that suggested he might be willing to straighten it up. He began by putting several books on a table, then grabbed some clothes off the floor, made an expression of disgust to signify they needed washing, and threw them over the back of the only chair in the room. Finally he looked about and shrugged again as if to say no one man could clean this room in the time we had together this afternoon.

I sat on the bed, which he had cleared for me, resting my back against a large poster of Muhammad Ali. William D. leaned on the desk and turned on the small lamp, then walked back to the door, closed it, and switched off the overhead bulb. Without looking at me, he walked toward the bed and sat down on the floor at my feet, leaning against the bed so that I could not see his face.

He began to talk about a girl in his class named Roberta whom he had walked home from school that day. Sheepishly he confessed to carrying her books, but when she had invited him upstairs to her house for something to eat he declined. He admitted being a little scared and using as an excuse that he had an appointment with a friend of his who is a professor at M.I.T. "She wasn't too impressed by that," William D. said, "so I gave her back her books." Apparently William D. helps Roberta in biology class, where she feels skittish about touching the animals. "Sometimes the boys have to help the girls," he told me.

"Roberta ever help you out in other classes?"

"Uh-uh. I do my own work. My father says it's best to figure things out by yourself." Then his voice became soft. "Every once in a while, though, she helps me with something, you know."

William D., however, was not that interested in Roberta. For once it was not I who seemed eager to speak about politics; today it was William D. who was waiting to tell of his reactions to the elections and to viewing the returns on television with his father. If our discussions together over the last months had had some cumulative effect, it was showing now. William D. had been pointing to this day despite our efforts to keep our previous conversations on daily happenings. To talk about politics during an election year was to keep one eye on November. Adrien too, I would learn later that afternoon, had been pointing to this day. Very likely, the many hours the children and I had spent together heightened our interest in the campaign, and while we rarely talked about outcomes, winning and losing, presumably, had been topics all along.

"I think it could have made a difference if the other guy won," William D. began. "I didn't a lot before, but I think so now. I'm glad about Brooke though. I wanted everyone to vote for him."

"Pretty many did," I pointed out.

"I know, but I wanted *everybody* to vote for him. Now we'll just have to see. He's got a lot of time to play with, old Nixon. Four years now and four years that were just over makes eight years. He could do a lot of stuff if he wanted to."

"Good stuff, you think?"

"Same stuff, I guess." I heard his voice drop. I imagined he was wearing that certain expression of disappointment I had seen so often. "I don't really know a lot of what goes on," he said in the tone of a religious confession. "Like last night, they were saying a lot of things I didn't understand. My father had to tell me what a lot of words meant, too. Part of the time I was just looking at all the numbers and adding them or subtracting them. I wasn't even listening to what was going on."

"I do that too, William D."

"You do?" He didn't seem especially surprised to learn this. "I did too. Sometimes I wanted them to be really close. Then sometimes I wanted one to win by lots and lots of votes. I was glad we didn't vote like the rest of the country. It makes you special in a way, don't you think so?"

"In a way, yes," I said.

"Yeah, that part was good. My father said, though, that even if black people aren't getting into politics it seems that it's about time they should be doing the announcing on TV. He kept changing the channels but we didn't see any black men announcing the news. All of 'em were white. They didn't even tell you how black folks voted. Like, before the election you always hear that black folks are going to vote for this or that, or that some candidate, you know, is trying to say things so that all the black folks in the cities all around will vote for him. But last night they didn't even once say anything about the way black folks were voting."

I told William D. that I had heard someone mention the black vote in a sample of large cities on one of the networks, but he dismissed my comment. Surely many analysts and careful observers of the elections had inspected the tabulations regarding black voting patterns, I continued. But I had overlooked the impression these data would make on a young man like William D. His accounts, moreover, prompted me to ask him direct questions about the elections I never imagined I would ask. In all the times we had spoken I had never inquired about his knowledge of facts, like how many senators and congressmen there are, or how many years the various elected officers serve, or what was the name of the person running against Senator Brooke in Massachusetts? Strangely, while I often subscribe to the notion that fundamental information about such a topic as politics may clutter up a young person's mind and disturb the more delicate creative processes, although I know this need not be true, I wanted in this case to ascertain the exact extent of his knowledge. Would others, too, I wondered, want to hear his responses to the traditional questions?

Sitting on William D.'s bed, I debated whether to ask him questions, as a schoolmaster might, while telling myself that William D. is fine no matter what he knows.

"You know how many senators there are, William D.?" I asked as casually as I could.

"A hundred," he answered in a flat way that seemed rather unlike him.

"Congressmen?"

"Lots. Almost five hundred. I forget."

"Most of 'em elected last night?"

"All of 'em."

"Senators *and* congressmen?"

"Just congressmen. Some senators."

"Serve two years, right?"

"Right. Senators six. Like old Brooke. Governors four, and don't ask me no more." He turned his head around and looked up at me curiously. "You being a schoolteacher or something today, man?"

"I guess I am, William D. Sorry about that." He did

know. And now that he has passed the "test," the questions seemed even more foolish and uninspiring.

"I got a question for *you* though," I heard him say.

"Okay. On politics?"

"Yeah, on politics."

"Go ahead."

"How many black congressmen they got?"

"My God," I groaned. I didn't know. "Can I guess?"

"Yeah." He was craning his neck to watch me.

"Eighteen," I guessed. He didn't say a word. "Is that right?" He remained silent. "Close?" I wondered. Still he didn't answer. He had an expression of sheer pleasure on his face. "Am I right or wrong? You got to tell, William D."

"Can't."

"What do you mean, you can't?"

" 'Cause I don't know."

"You don't know?"

"No."

"Then why'd you ask me?"

" 'Cause I *wanted* to know," he answered.

"You mean you weren't testing me?"

"No. I wasn't. Honest. Why would I be testing you?" He sounded puzzled. "I just wanted to know. You know everything like that so I thought I'd ask you."

"It's a damned reasonable question and we're going to find out. Will your dad know?"

"Probably," he replied. "But see, they didn't say anything last night on television. They don't tell you that. I wanted to know but they didn't say, so I thought you would know. Nobody knows. My mother didn't know either. I didn't get to ask my teacher."

William D. was silent. He had turned back to gaze at the

floor and the objects surrounding him. His legs were jammed under the dresser and he was breathing deeply.

"You sleeping, William D.?" I kidded him.

"Nah. Why, you tired?"

"Nope. I'll bet old McGovern is though," I said, hoping to touch one last political base before I left.

"That's the only part that makes me really sad, man. All that work he did. All that work. He was just running, running, running, every day there, wasn't he? And what's he got to show for it now? Nothing. Nothing at all. Nobody wants to have anything to do with a cat who loses. Man, I don't think I could ever do that. All that work and you can't show nothing to anyone. Maybe they could make the guy who loses the Vice President. He deserves it. I feel bad for the guy." William D. scratched his head and held his hands together in his lap. "What I learned from old 'Govern is that wanting to be something like that takes a whole lot of work. Don't seem worth it though to me if you lose. You got to have something when you're finished and he ain't got anybody or anything. 'Cept all his money. I used to think, you know, that just having all that money would be enough. But you see a guy like him, he isn't doing it for the money. Can't be. He's got all he needs. So why's he do it? Must be other reasons. Maybe it's 'cause he really wants to do some good things. I don't know. Beats me. Strange, this dude wanting all that when he doesn't really need it." Then in the same breath he asked, "Think you might run for something, Tom?"

"No. I don't think so," I answered.

"Me neither."

"But I thought you said you were thinking of running someday. Is that thought all gone?"

"After last night, you kidding me? Sure, it's gone. I ain't

ready to work that hard and end up with *nothing*. You got to be crazy. The dude was lucky he didn't get himself killed too. No sir, no President's house for me."

"William D.," I started, leaning over his shoulder so that I could see at least the side of his face, "you're holding something back. Election make you sad?"

"No, not really."

"I think it did," I persisted. "Want to talk about it?" I heard myself carrying on like a psychotherapist.

"I don't know," he said.

"Try me."

"I ain't got much to say, 'cepting I thought that maybe things would change. That's all. Last night I told my mother and father that things were really going to change for us. I was wishing for them to change, you know. I don't know this dude 'Govern from anyone else. I just heard a lot of talk, like at the church and that place where my dad goes . . ."

"Job training center?"

"Yeah, that maybe the President has it in for poor folks, and black folks, and that I guess they need to get money from him and he doesn't give it to 'em, except there's another word they used." He was pointing his finger in space above his head as if he were trying to read some invisible print.

"Veto the bills, you mean?"

"Yeah. Veto. Like, he kills 'em. Isn't that what it means?"

"Yes. The President has the power to stop the passage of bills, although the Congress may overrule him in some cases."

"But they don't with us," he sighed. "Well, anyway, they were counting on the money but they aren't probably going to get it now. So there's going to be no park for kids on Lambert Field, and no day-care centers, which means I either have to baby-sit all the time or my mother can't get a job, and probably all their other plans aren't going to come true either."

"You follow this political stuff very closely, don't you, William D.?" I remarked. I had heard, too, the sound of betrayal in his words that he meant for me to hear.

"I just listen to them talking about what they're going to do if they get all the money. All the kids, like, we ask them every time we go down there, 'Are you getting it? Are you getting it?' And they always use these big words on us and try to explain how it works. But if you ask me, all they're saying is that they don't have the money and they aren't going to get it. I don't see why they just can't go down there and ask for it themselves. Why they keeping us waiting for things to happen somewhere? Everybody's always *waiting* for things to be happening to 'em. They ain't going to get nothing that way."

"But you thought that if McGovern got elected last night things might change somehow, and that those people would get the money?"

"I thought that, yeah." His answer was rimmed with shame. I could feel him wanting to add the disclaimer, But what do children know, after all? Children hope for little things as well as big things, and can't stand the idea of conditions being the same all the time. Children think a new man will make different things happen, and then the children and their families will be different too. What had his mother said to me earlier? "Things don't suddenly get any better having this new man around; they probably don't get any worse either. Everything stays just about the same. Families make things stay just about the way they were, I suppose, and the governments do too. The country goes on."

"You got to hope that," I heard William D. say. "Four years now we got to wait. But old Brooke, he doesn't work again until six years."

"I wouldn't say he doesn't *work* for six years," I corrected him good-naturedly.

William D. laughed. "Yeah. He better work. We got him in there to work. He's going to see lots of trouble if he doesn't work for us. All the people around here, anyway, would take a trip down there to Washington and *make* him work if he doesn't."

"You think they would, eh?"

"Sure thing they would. I *know* they would. He's got to work now. All of 'em got to go back to work for us now. No more partying around. No more late nights playing in the streets, whooping it up with their music and all the booze." He was grinning and preparing to stand up. "No more running around," he sang. "Everybody's got to go back to work." He pronounced the words very carefully.

A certain fantasy was ending for us both, and for other people too, I imagined as we entered the hall and walked the few steps to the living room. Just the slightest remnant of a giant wish had remained on this day following the elections. It was as if an enormous balloon had exploded over America, dropping its pieces in the bedroom of a Boston schoolboy. For an instant he had gathered the tattered pieces and tried, as children do, to blow a little bubble from the remains. Now he had given it up.

When we reached the living room Mrs. Williams was not there.

"Hey, Mom, Tom's going," William D. yelled out when he saw the room empty.

There are two kinds of approaches to losing in politics, I

thought, walking to the front door with William D. There is poetic death and furious withdrawal. No, there is a third: betrayal; a child's sense of having been betrayed mixed with the awareness that it is childish to feel this way. This was the special connection William D. had made with Washington and Sioux Falls, South Dakota — particularly Sioux Falls, where Senator McGovern's concession speech was delivered. What I concluded from his tone and posture, slouched as he had been on the floor, preferring not to face me, was that politics is adult business about which children presumably get to know some little measure. Political talk belongs in the discussions children overhear their parents having. There is nothing especially secretive about these discussions, but believing, perhaps, that children might be bored by them, parents may hold them at night when the children are in bed. And so, when the adults make their final decisions, as they had yesterday, the children are left with their sentiments, and a renewed understanding that they have no right to feel discouraged or betrayed, as if that understanding really mattered. This was the first time in more than a year of political talks with William D. that he actually communicated a feeling of shame for having been involved or implicated in the political world about which we spoke.

At the front door, I put my hand on his shoulder. He didn't move or acknowledge my gesture in any way. "So long, Mrs. Williams," I shouted in the direction of the kitchen.

"So long yourself," came her reply. "Come back and see us soon."

"I will. Thanks."

"Does the election mean you're all through coming around?" she shouted.

"No ma'am. Just starting," I shouted back, looking at

William D. so that he would know my message was meant for him as well.

"That's cool too," I heard her say. "And shut that door when you leave, Mr. Professor."

"I will. I will."

William D. barely smiled at the recollection of my clowning with the lock earlier that afternoon.

"I'll be back in a week," I said to him. "We'll talk about whatever you want. Take care of yourself, man. Call me if you want to."

"It's going to be cold in a week," he replied sternly.

"I know. I'll bundle up." I grinned. "I don't think I'm ready to freeze yet. Okay?"

"Okay."

I couldn't get him to smile. "See you then, William D.," I said soberly. "Week from today, all right?"

"Okay."

"Right after school?"

"Okay." He held the door open for me and closed it gently the instant I was outside in the dark chilled stairwell.

Chapter 8

TWENTY MINUTES after leaving the Williamses' home I arrived at the Kellers'. While the two families live only eight blocks apart, I had to sit in the car awhile before making my way over to the Kellers'. No one could know, of course, when I finished at one home and left for the other, but something caused me to hesitate, if only to let one thing end before commencing the next.

The rain continued to fall, and the temperature was noticeably colder than before. Now in the late afternoon it was getting darker. I badly wanted to break my appointment with Adrien and be inside my own home, where it would be warm and comfortable. I had had enough for one day. I no longer wanted to be in this community. I no longer wanted to listen to the words of these children. I could visualize the Keller home, which I have visited so many times, and Adrien — perhaps even guess what she was wearing. I could conjure up, too, the self-consciousness I continue to feel in her home as well as in the other homes I visit in these blocks. I am not totally myself in these homes is what I thought sitting alone in the car peering out at the phone booth across the street from the Williams apartment. I am not free here and surely these families are not free with me, and this fact colors our conversations and friendships.

The anticipation of just starting with Adrien today, breaking the ice, made it seem a momentous, even onerous chore.

Again we would have to warm up to one another and to this business of politics and her feelings about the elections. Again we would have to make one another feel at ease, despite the differences between us. I was not up to confronting her; I was not up to facing myself in her presence. And the weather did not help any.

No one is shocked to learn that a tippleman in a mine or a feeder on an assembly line might get bored and irritated with his work. But most people, probably, do not like to hear of the irritability and feeling of dullness that comes over teachers, guidance counselors, and psychotherapists. And then, I announced to myself parking the car in the alley adjoining the Kellers' apartment building, there remains the burden of psychological sophistication. How much of this irritability and dullness, this unwillingness to go on, and this sudden intense reaction to the dreary weather is caused by William D., the elections, my leaving him, his leaving me? If it is the impact of this boy on me that makes this next meeting with Adrien so trying, then how do I quickly rid my mind of this impact and prepare myself wholly to receive her?

I was dripping with water when I reached the Kellers' entryway. Adrien met me at the door of the apartment. Shoeless as usual, she was dressed in a red sweatshirt and well-worn jeans. A picture of a man's face adorned the sweatshirt but I did not recognize him at first.

"Who's that?" I pointed at her, taking off my wet coat and hanging it over the doorknob.

"I don't know. I think he's a baseball player," Adrien replied, smiling at the sight of my disheveled appearance.

"Let me see."

She stretched out the shirt front so that I now could recognize Henry Aaron, the baseball player.

"Hey, that's Hank Aaron," I cried out, thinking about ways to break the ice and feeling the self-consciousness return.

"You know him?" she asked, somewhat amazed.

"Hammerin' Hank? Everybody knows Hammerin' Hank. Big number forty-four for Atlanta? Of course I do."

"Oh yeah?" More than bewildered, she seemed a trifle irritated by my enthusiasm.

"Adrien, you've got to be kidding me. You really don't know Hank Aaron?"

"No. And I sure don't know also what you're getting so excited about with this crummy sweatshirt which doesn't even belong to me."

"I'm excited by Hank Aaron." I was calming down, forcing myself into the role she expected of me. "He's a great baseball player. I thought you knew him."

"I know Reggie Smith, and Reggie Jackson, and Reggie . . . somebody else. And Jackie Robinson."

"And Jackie Robinson," I repeated softly, trying to find the energy for our work.

"He died," she said.

"Yes, I know."

"He was a great baseball player too."

"Was he ever. He was, in a way, all of America when I was a kid. Can you understand that, Adrien?"

"Uh-uh, not really. I know that a lot of people liked him. He was the first Negro baseball player too."

Adrien had had her fill of baseball, but her irritability helped me to get back on normal ground with her. We didn't meet in the kitchen today. Instead, we stayed in the living room, where I sat on the couch on which her mother had sat that hot afternoon when she told me of the fire she had watched as a child. Adrien sat in the green easy chair.

It was hard to begin the conversation, just as it is hard to in-
itiate all the other conversations like this one. I know what
I want to ask, but even if I feel certain that the other person
is eager to tell me something, I cannot open the discussion,
somehow, without a minor struggle. The resistance suggests
an ambivalence about using the other person in some way.
Even if she is willing to share her history or experiences, I
am diffident in the beginning. If she could just produce
something without my having to prompt her it would be
better. If Adrien, for example, could now say, "Well, here's
a run-down on my post-election thoughts . . ." In fact, she
was saying nothing.

Her eyes focused on the floor. She knew that I was studying her.

"You want to talk about some political stuff?" I asked as
gently as I could.

"Hmm."

"Nixon winning?"

"No."

"McGovern losing? Something else?"

"Him losing maybe."

"It was quite a crunch," I said.

"I thought it was awful. I cried last night," she said without glancing up. "I felt real bad for him. Everybody was
watching him and listening to him all those months, and
now it's — I don't know. It's like he died last night."

"I hope he didn't die."

"Well, maybe not really died, but it was *like* he died."

I recalled Mrs. Keller speaking once about the candidates
competing at a time when the slurs and innuendoes had
reached their highest point. "Two men, two grown men
going after each other like they are just now," she had said,
"makes you wonder what it's all coming to. My, my, my,

what they say about each other. Do you listen to it? Practically not out of bed in the morning and they're already up and screaming at each other about one thing or another. It's hard to see sometimes how either man could get himself settled down and be a sober man on the job. All that yelling and fighting over what, I'd like to know? To have all that power, I suppose. Seems to me the more they talk, the less they have to do for anybody."

I had told Mrs. Keller that Mrs. Williams, whom she knew slightly, had remarked that most likely Nixon and McGovern poked their jibes at one another as a way of not ever having to say anything substantial on any issue.

"Amen" had been Mrs. Keller's response. Her face had lit up and her words suddenly took on the sounds, as they did from time to time, of those regions of the rural South where she was raised, and where her parents and grandparents lived their entire lives. "Ain't that ever the case," she said closing her eyes as if dreaming of the voices of long ago. "Like two little boys whipping themselves up into this great big huff out behind the barn so they can't hear their mother calling for them to come in and finish their chores."

"You said you cried, Adrien?"

"Yes. Last night. I felt so badly for him." She hadn't mentioned Senator McGovern by name. "I felt like if he wasn't going to win, he wasn't going to live either, and that maybe I'd get up this morning and find out that he died."

"Like, of a broken heart?"

"Something like that," she replied in earnest. "I had a dream about him last night too. I think it was last night. I don't remember exactly."

"Want to tell me?"

"He came to our house, in the dream." She looked at me to see whether I had understood. I nodded as a psychotherapist might. "Only my mother and me and him were here. We all sat down in my bedroom. He was real uncomfortable, I remember, 'cause he was real tall. Real tall, you know, like a basketball player. He kept hitting his head. It was really him too. I saw his face when he came in but he sure looked uncomfortable trying to sit someplace in my room. Then he says, 'I've been speaking with your father and your grandparents, Adrien, and they all want you to know that they love you very, very much.' And then he says, 'I'm not really coming here to ask you and your mother to vote for me. You will have to make up your own mind about that. I just wanted to make a special visit to give you that message.' Then he looked right at me and says, 'I know, Adrien, that you really love your father very much, and that makes me happy knowing it. It makes my wife happy too, and all our children too. You see, we like to see all the children in America happy.'" Adrien no longer hunted for my reactions to her dream.

"What else did he say now?" she prodded herself. "Let me think. Oh yes, I remember now. He was going to leave, I remember that. He almost hit his head on the top of the door, you know, and we, my mother and me, we both said, 'Look out, be careful,' you know, so he didn't hit his head. Then he turned around to look at us, holding his head like he'd hit it only we knew he didn't. Then he says, 'That was a very close call. I would have hit my head on that door for sure if you two hadn't warned me.' He was looking right at us then. 'So I thank you,' he goes. 'I thank you ladies very much. You see, you've helped me. And now I want to help you.' Then he reaches into his pocket and pulls out this big envelope and gives it to my mother, and he says, 'Or would you like me to give it to your oldest daughter here?' And my mother says, 'No, I'll take it, Mr. Senator.' That's what she

called him in the dream: Mr. Senator. So he gives her the
envelope and she opens it very slowly. All the time now, in
the dream, I'm thinking that I know what he's brought for
us. I mean, I'm not awake or anything but I can see what
the envelope looks like and I think he may be the President,
which means he can do anything he wants, just about, so I
figure out that he's got all the insurance money. I figure
that my mother knows what it is too, 'cause she's just smiling
there looking happier, you know, than she looks when I'm
not dreaming." Adrien and I moved in our places. I felt
chilled. She glanced quickly at me, fearing that I might
have wanted to stand up.

"Well, so she reaches into the envelope and I'm getting
real excited, and don't you know she pulls out this stupid little, like, baby's animal. It's this little tiger doll with a long
tail. It's all yellow or gold with black spots and whiskers.
It's really a silly, dumb-looking thing. I mean, it's really
like what happens in dreams because the envelope was small,
you know, and flat." She clapped her hands together. "But
this little tiger animal was inside."

"What'd you think then?"

"Well, Senator McGovern was really happy. It was like he
really thought that's what we wanted, but I was disappointed. I think I even wanted to take it from my mother
and hit him with it. But I didn't. I thought it was, you
know . . ."

"Your father's insurance money."

"Yeah. But it wasn't. It was this stupid old doll-like thing
in there. I was really disappointed. So I look over at my
mother feeling pretty sure she's going to be real disappointed too, and what do you think? She's holding the doll
with both arms and squeezing it." Adrien embraced the imaginary tiger. "She's even crying. And Senator McGovern,

he's real happy, like he gave us the greatest present in the world he could. My mother's crying 'cause she's so excited, and I'm mad, you know. I just want to take that thing and hit him on the head with it, over and over again."

"You were that disappointed."

"Man, I was *so* disappointed. It's kind of a double thing too. I was disappointed it wasn't the money he brought us. That's number one. And number two, I felt my mother was putting on this big act for the man so he would think she really digs him, but I know she doesn't. She was just afraid to tell him what she really thinks. So I was mad at *her* too." Adrien's dream had ended.

"That's some dream, Glide."

"Boy, was I glad to wake up. I sat up in bed, you know, like you do when you have dreams like that, and looked all around. First thing I saw was Arthur walking out of the bathroom in the hall pulling his pants up. Crazy dream. Maybe I'm going crazy!"

"It's kind of a rich dream, I'd say."

"Well, it's something about the elections anyway," she said. "Maybe I dreamed it for you 'cause I knew you would be coming today, and I've been thinking about the elections, politics and stuff, and what we would talk about, but I don't know anymore." Adrien was sitting in a more erect position than usual. Normally she slouched in a chair or rested much of her weight on the table when we sat face to face in the kitchen. Today, however, she carried herself differently, which made it seem as if she wanted to be done with the whole matter of politics.

"I feel sorry for Mr. McGovern," she said finally, seeing I had nothing in particular to ask. "That's one thing anyway. I feel sorry for him."

"I suppose a lot of people do."

"You think Nixon can do anything he wants to now? He can't ever lose again, right?"

"That's right."

"Well, does that mean he can do anything?"

"I don't think he can do *anything*," I answered. "Heaven only knows what a man with that much power can do, though."

"Know what I want him to do?" she asked.

"What?"

"Three things. I got them written down." Adrien stretched her legs out in front of her so that she could shove her hand into the right front pocket of her jeans. On a wrinkled scrap of paper I saw that she had made some jottings. "I wrote this in school today and tore it out of my notebook. It's for you."

Concentrating on pulling the paper out of her pocket without ripping it, she was unaware of how important the note was to me.

"Okay now." Adrien carefully stretched out the paper and laid it on her thigh. "One thing is he's got to lower all the prices. We can't eat as much as we need to 'cause the food's going up. We used to rely on chicken but even that's too high now. I do all the shopping, you know, so I keep watching the prices."

I nodded yes, and recalled how frightened she had been by the plans for a food boycott at the Greenough Mart.

"So that's number one," she said. "Then, after they do what they have to do with the food prices, they got to promise to solve the crime problem."

"Got any details on that?" I asked.

"Details?"

"In your notes?"

"Like what?"

"Well, you know, what do you want them to do?"

"No. I mean, they got their ways. I just don't want to be robbed no more."

Her mother's lecture several months before had not settled Adrien's concern about crime, and especially that robbery; Adrien's point number two attested to this. "Now that it's Nixon again," she said, studying her small list of items, "I hope he'll do something to stop crime. It really gets me angry that someone can come into your home and take things. I only hope that if we get robbed again I won't be here. That's what really makes me more scared than anything. William D. once told me that if you catch the robbers in the act, like right when they're taking something, they'll probably run out of the room and jump through a window or something, but I'm not so sure about that. I mean, it would be my luck that if I saw 'em they'd hit me on the head, or something worse too. William D., though, he says I'm crazy. I told him all this once, right after we were robbed the last time, and he said I got my robbers and my murderers mixed up. That doesn't help a person, you know, saying things like that. Well, anyway, that's my number two. They got to do something about crime."

We had reached Adrien's third point. She was already rolling up the slip of paper containing her list of items and placing it in the ashtray.

"Guess what it is," she said to me, grinning.

I thought for a moment, trying to decide what she would consider so important.

"School," I announced finally. "Desegregation of schools."

"No," she replied, not yet ready to reveal the mystery.

"Not school, eh? Guaranteed family income?"

"No."

"You know what that means though, right?"

"Of course."

"Was it important in the elections?"

She was laughing aloud. "See, I didn't know about *him*" — she pulled the front of her sweatshirt out for me — "but you don't know *this*."

"I quit. Show me the damn piece of paper." I reached for the ashtray expecting her to stop me, but she remained perfectly still. It took a moment to unwad the paper. Even when the sheet was as smooth as I could get it, her handwriting was difficult to read among the wrinkles. "To tell Tom" was written across the top of the page; the numbers 1, 2, and 3 occupied the left margin. Opposite 3 she had written, "Dear God, and Nixon too, stop all the wars. Forever."

"Stop all the wars," I recited.

"Forever," she added. "Don't forget the *forever*. No more wars. He's going to stop this one now, isn't he?"

"That's what they say," I answered.

"But then will there be another one somewhere?"

"God, I hope not."

"Me neither. My mother says there will always be a war somewhere in the world. I think I agree with her. But maybe soon there won't be any more wars. I'm not even sure where this war is. It's a long way from here, isn't it?"

"Very long."

"I heard a man say once that if it weren't for all these wars a lot of folks would never get to travel anywhere. Like, he said that if it wasn't for some war he was in — Korea, I think — that he wouldn't have gotten to go to Japan. So that's the good part of the wars. But there are too many bad parts. Anyway, how come you couldn't think of what my number three was?"

"I don't know, Adrien. I didn't think, because of your age, I suppose, that the war would matter as much as some of the other things we've spoken about. You know what I mean?"

"Not really," she answered thoughtfully. "All the kids I know talk about the war. They say we shouldn't be there. Some of the boys are worried there will still be a war when they're old enough to go."

"Do they talk about not going?" I wondered.

"No. They *have* to go to the army or navy. But I don't know what else they think about."

The matter of the draft did not excite Adrien until she was able to turn her ideas away from military recruitment to the boys she knew who would someday enter the army. She reasoned that if wars would end, then the army or navy would offer decent enough jobs. It was not until she used the phrase "What I don't like is that it's *young* boys who go" that her feelings of betrayal and bitterness finally erupted. The idea that *old* people decide to make wars and send young people to do the fighting aroused her anger. "If I don't like what other eleven-year-old kids are doing," she said, "I should be able to start *my* war with them. But if fifty- and sixty-year-old people don't like each other, then *they* should fight. Not me!

"Sometimes I pretend, you know, that the soldiers and everybody aren't really dead. Like, after the war is over, everybody can stand up again and walk around and do things like they were doing before."

"Like a children's game."

"Yeah. It's only pretending, but it's a better way to think about it. Otherwise you have to keep telling yourself that they're really dead, and that they're never coming back." Adrien looked at me to see whether I had caught all the implications she intended. I wanted to say, Like your father. She examined her hands, looking especially hard at her left thumb as though a special pain were suddenly located there. "Wars are funny. People shooting people they can't even see. And the soldiers lying out in the cold grass in those holes of theirs, or walking around in all that mud." She shuddered. "It's awful. When I see the pictures they show on television I'm really glad I'm not a boy. I wouldn't ever want to go there. But lots of kids I know want to go. They think it's cool being in the army, wearing the uniforms, you know, and walking around like you're really somebody important. That's not the way I'd like to be important though. Boys can do that. I'd rather be a housewife."

"Or a lawyer," I interjected. She didn't understand my reference at first.

"Oh yeah. A lawyer. You're still on that kick of me being a lawyer, aren't you?"

"Sure, why not?"

"You got to be crazy, man. Can you see me being a lawyer, bringing people into the courtroom and all, and sending them to jail? Folks around here" — she laughed — "are the ones who *go* to jail, not the ones that try to keep people *out* of jail. Next thing you'll be telling me is I ought to go in the army and become a general or something."

"No, I won't suggest that."

"Just law, eh? But not the army?"

"Probably not."

"Army makes a nice life for lots of folks, you know," she said.

"Yes, I realize that."

"Men *and* women are going into the army, you know?"

"I know that too, Adrien."

"So what's wrong with me going into the army then? They got more folks like me in there than they do trying to make it to be a lawyer."

"True. That's true too. Maybe it's because I got a prefer-
ence for the law over the military." I assumed, naturally,
that she would agree.

"Maybe so, but maybe, too, rich folks like you are lawyers
and poor folks like me go into the army." She was biting her
lower lip.

I changed the subject and asked her what she thought of a
volunteer army.

"There has to be an army," she answered dutifully, willing
to leave our lawyer-soldier debate. "Everyone knows that.
We have lots of enemies so we need to make sure they don't
come here and attack us."

"Who are our enemies, Adrien?" I was still feeling uncomfortable after her announcement that some people become lawyers and others become soldiers.

"China, I guess. Maybe the Russians too. I'm not sure
about them, but we must have a lot of enemies all over the
place." She looked around the room as if to be certain we
were alone.

"Is Arthur in the house?" I asked.

"I don't think so." She seemed puzzled. "I don't remember now whether he came in or not. ARTHUR KELLER,
YOU THERE?" she yelled. We waited. Everything was
silent. "ARTHUR KELLER, YOU HOME?" she yelled
again.

"NO, I'M NOT HOME" came the response from the bedroom beyond the kitchen.

Adrien giggled with delight. "GOOD," she yelled back.
"NOW I CAN TALK ABOUT YOU BEHIND YOUR
BACK."

"HELL YOU CAN," he yelled out. "DON'T WANT
NOBODY TALKING ABOUT ME OUT THERE."

Adrien was smiling and watching me to see whether I enjoyed her brother as much as she did. "He's crazy, that boy,"

she said. "Don't want anybody talking out here about him. You hear that?" Just then we heard an enormous crash coming from the rear of the apartment.

"What the — WHAT HAPPENED, ARTHUR? HUH? YOU ALL RIGHT BACK THERE?"

"DOOR FELL OFF," he yelled back angrily. "SAME DAMN DOOR FALLS OFF ALL THE TIME. I HATE THIS HOUSE!"

"SHUT YOUR MOUTH AND FIX IT," Adrien shouted without moving. We heard nothing.

"FIX IT YOURSELF," he yelled back at last. There was a pause. "I HATE YOU TOO, ADRIEN!"

"ME TOO," she snapped back. Then to me she said, "If he didn't want to go into the army it'd be all right with me. I could understand that maybe he's afraid, or maybe he doesn't like wars any more than I do. But I'd probably tell him that he *should* go because grown-up men have to go."

"So what do you think about those men who left the country rather than be in the army?"

Adrien hesitated a long time before answering. She was giving the question serious thought.

"Now, this is going to sound wrong 'cause I haven't got it all worked out, but . . . I think that if a man doesn't want to fight he shouldn't have to 'cause there could be lots of reasons for not wanting to. He could be afraid, or he could think that wars are stupid. But now, since someone has to take his place, I think he has to do something to make it up. Otherwise everybody would quit. They shouldn't punish him, like put him in jail or nothing like that, but no one can go around thinking he can just quit if he wants to. Besides, in this country everybody knows who has to do the dirty work when people quit. It's always the same people who have to do it. My older brother, Quintin, says black boys can't quit the army 'cause they have no place to go and hide. He says he may quit it, maybe, but first he's got to see what the army's like. He thinks he'll make pretty good money working in it too."

"So he'll go?"

"I guess so."

"And Arthur?"

Adrien smiled. "I hope he doesn't go, but I guess he'll go too. Maybe they'll give him a break 'cause he had a brother who went and he doesn't have a father. One person in each family should go, I think, but not all of them. Girls should go too. They got lots of jobs in the army girls could do."

"Would you go?"

"No sir. I think it would be terrible. Spending all that time just learning how to kill people. I don't need any of that. If I want to learn that" — she grinned — "all I got to do is turn on the television over there. They'll teach me that. I don't even need to get out of my chair. Course if you do go in the army, like I was saying before, you get to travel."

The tone of both our voices had softened. Everything about the room, too, gradually was softening, becoming somehow ephemeral. The idea of her traveling and escaping from her surroundings and imagination told of a fantasy she harbored. Adrien wanted to move away from talk of the army, the fright of killing, a brother dying, a father dying. And I wanted to encourage this flight of hers, believing that its expression would make possible the birth of a new image, a statement perhaps of her philosophy, perhaps a testimony or a prayer.

"Where would you like to travel, Adrien?"

"Oh, I don't know," she answered dreamily. "Let's see. I've never been out of Massachusetts, I don't think. So, maybe I could go to Texas. Or Florida. Or I'd like to see California too. There's a boy in my class, Carris, who lived in California when he was little. San Diego, which is in California, right?"

"Right. Southern part."

"Yeah, he was telling us all about it once. Sun's always shining there, he said. But they got bad weather too, although not like here, I'll bet." We both looked toward the window. The rain continued to fall and one could almost see the weather turning colder.

"Some of the kids in my class saw this television show," Adrien was saying, "where they asked these children how many of them had ever been on a plane. About half of them, the man said. No one in my class has been on a plane. My teacher said she was on twice. I was on a train once when we went somewhere, I don't remember where, but that was the only time."

"Where are you now?" I asked.

"San Diego." She closed her eyes.

"What's it like?"

"Pretty. And hot."

"Lots of people there?"

"Not too many."

"Can you go swimming?"

"Hmm."

"Play sports too?"

"Hmm."

"What else?"

"Let me see. Music."

"Good stuff?"

"Real good. I'm having dinner too."

"Food taste good?"

"Yeah. And there's lots of it." She opened her eyes. "I

was really there. You know that? I was really dreaming I was there. It was like I was in that city, 'cause I could see it." She sounded excited, not only by the visions, but by her ability to ignite her imagination. "That was really fun."

"Better than talking about war," I suggested.

"You can say that again. Nothing good about that. Hey, let's see, did I have more to tell you about that war business, besides my surprise thing?"

"What's that?"

"Hold on, now, I'll be with you in a second. I just got to sort through my thoughts here. I told you I want an army and that poor folks fill in when the rich boys go away. Did I say something about the army turning all these older boys into, like, civilian soldiers?"

"No."

"Well, they are. You know all about that. They come back and keep their guns in their houses."

"So what do you think about that?"

"I don't know. The army can't have it both ways, like my brother says. If they teach you how to kill, they can't always be so sure when and where you're going to kill. That's what Quintin says, anyway. Once they know how to do it, there's no saying when it's going to happen again. At least they got their guns now. They got their protection with them anyway."

I was troubled by this mood of Adrien's. Many of us argue for revolutionary types of ideas. We say something like "There's nothing salvageable here so let's just tear the whole thing down and start from scratch." We may not be advocating the destruction of institutions, but it is, nevertheless, a revolutionary rather than reformist perspective. But now, when Adrien reminds me again that revolution also implies people killing people, the idea of revolution becomes far less capricious, and frightening, even if one believes in its inevitability.

The literature on revolution, the scenes of trials of so-called revolutionaries, the sight of young people in the streets holding out leaflets, and words like "struggle," "class conflict," "overthrow" rushed through my mind making it impossible for me to settle my feelings on any one thing. Perhaps Adrien wished now to add something to what she had said, qualify a statement, or even totally reorder her thoughts.

As I studied her face, hunting, I suppose, for signs of ambivalence or open animosity, something simple and decisive gradually surfaced: I don't want to be the enemy of this child or her family.

"You think there will be a real revolution someday, Adrien?"

"Maybe. Maybe so," she replied thoughtfully. "Never can tell."

"Killing and all, huh?"

"Maybe that too." Her tone was free of emotion and her way seemed strong and sure. When people talk of power, they appear to possess power. It suffuses their blood and emerges in their language and demeanor. They feel it. Adrien lurched back in the easy chair with a purposeful force, then bounced back to an erect position. "I want to tell you something."

"Your surprise?"

"Yeah. It's real simple, but it's scary too."

I had a vision suddenly of the young woman Marlene, Adrien's friend, who had become pregnant at the age of fourteen. Adrien had laughed at her own description of this young woman, although the image of Marlene's pregnancy had frightened her as well. "Like one half of her was a girl, you know," she had said, "and the other half was real old. An old lady." We had passed now from wars to revolution to pregnancy. That is, I had taken it to this last point. "What is it, Glide? Can I help?"

"I hope so. It's a dream, like. Not the kind when you're sleeping, but the kind when you're awake and sitting in class, or maybe waiting for the oven to get warm."

"A daydream."

"Yeah. A surprise daydream."

I felt relief.

"It's very cold outside," she began. "The wind is going *sshhh-sshhh*. People are walking real slowly, and it's starting to get dark. It's winter. Like it could be today, although it's never any real day. Then all of a sudden it gets very quiet. Nobody's talking anymore. Everybody's moving real slowly, but nobody's making any sound." Her eyes were closed. "Everything is turning gray and this light purple color. People, and their clothes, and the streets and the houses are all gray and purple. And the wind keeps going *sshhh-sshhh*. Then, somewhere, a person falls over. I never see him, because when I go to see him, 'cause I know it's going to happen, it's already happened. Anyway, he falls over, and he's dead. Maybe he's even a soldier but I'm not sure. He's gray and purple too. And when he falls he hits someone else and this man falls over too. And then he hits someone and he falls, and over and over again people just fall and die and touch someone else who falls and dies. I see people in elevators dying, one after the other, and on fields and, like, walking up the stairs or down the stairs in the trolley station. Everybody's just falling, very quietly. They don't cry or yell, they just fall over, and when they do, they touch someone and then they die. The wind is blowing this way, you know, *sshhh,* and the land is very flat and sandy. It's real strange.

Pretty soon I know that people are dying across the ocean too, like on boats and planes and trains. They just keep falling over, one by one. The colors never change. Just gray and purple. But when the last person on the earth dies, the wind stops and the colors go out. Like candles. There's no more light, and I know that everyone in the world is dead."

At last she opened her eyes. Neither of us said anything. We could hear Arthur making repairs in the bedroom.

"Sshhh," I whispered.

"Sshhh," she answered, smiling. Strange how her face, after these words, showed hope. "So please," she was saying, pointing to the crumpled piece of paper that I still held, "let there be no more wars forever, or there will be no more people, and no more colors, and no more wind . . ."

Chapter 9

THIS BOOK IS PREDICATED on a simple irony. Of all the people to be a subject of a study of political awareness and sensitivity, we have chosen poor black children who are among the most oppressed groups in America. Yet despite the oppression, their age, their lack of rights, and their conceptions of themselves and their parents formed in part by *our* actions, visions, and analyses, these children continue to learn about politics and the system of political relationships that govern their lives.

In writing about this group of children, I constantly feel the predisposition to overromanticize them, or at least the two children whose words fill this book. At the very least, I feel a need for something with which to counteract the reality of their circumstances. Merely to raise this problem, however, and reveal my awareness of it in no way resolves the dangers of overromanticizing anyone's life. I know that I have invested feelings in Adrien and William D., as well as indulged in sharing my own thoughts when it might have been "better" to "stand back" and assume an air of objectivity, or the traditional role of "outside" observer. Indeed one might think, given the disparities between my life and the lives of these children, that an outsider's role would be easily assumed.

The withholding of feelings, both in discussions with the children and in writing, is something with which I continually struggle. If there is a rule about this form of research, it might be reduced to something as simple as *pay attention*. Pay attention to what the child says and does and feels; pay attention to the scene, the spaces, streets, rooms, textures, colors and lighting; pay attention to what is evoked by these conversations and perceptions, particularly when one's mind wanders so very far away; and finally, pay attention to the responses of those who might, through one's work, hear these children. As many writers have suggested, paying attention implies an openness. It is not any special or metaphysical kind of openness, but merely a watch on oneself, a self-consciousness, a belief that everything one takes in from the outside and experiences within one's own interior is worthy of consideration and essential for understanding and honoring those whom one encounters.

The expression of the investigator's feelings, moreover, contributes to the reality of the situation, for the situation itself is in part composed of the investigator. It is through the investigator that one hears these children. So, like the children and their parents, the reader too wants to know whether the investigator can be trusted. Who is this person who will be listening to the children and reporting their words and experiences?

Each of us knows the many roles situations demand that we play. We sense too the qualitative shifts in personality that these situations generate. We come away from one home and say, I was uncomfortable there, I was not myself. We come away from another home and report feeling free to be the persons we believe we genuinely are. In the Williams and Keller homes I do not, as I have suggested, feel free to say things I may let myself say elsewhere. If for no other reason, the asymmetry in my friendships with these families makes us all feel the weightiness of observation and constant self-regard. In our giving to one another we also hold back; although in our holding back we give each other still another part of ourselves, a part with which we may or may not be satisfied.

Both sides, the families and the investigator, observe new selves emerging, the selves that "belong" to this special situation. On the one hand, Mrs. Williams remarks on William D.'s "good manners" and articulate ways when he is with me. On the other hand, I see myself at times bumbling, groping for words, for a good question or generous response, in a manner I feel to be discrepant from my manner at other times. I find myself, too, coming upon new words just as William D. and Adrien find whole new families of words and images which they feel to be inappropriate for school but somehow right for me. So we are all on our guard, watching each other, and most especially watching ourselves watching each other. And in our changing ways, we seek to be respectful and caring of one another, and try not to be inhibited by the different circumstances of our lives or by the different appearances of our bodies.

One result of this brand of work, then, is to consecrate a series of settings and relationships that transcends the settings and forms of relationships normally experienced by the participants. Thus, William D. softens the lighting in his bedroom when we speak, and Adrien prepares the kitchen table in a way that suggests intimacy. All of us think of one another as "that special friend," and work to attain the feelings of mutual recognition, mutual acknowledgment.

Now, there is an important point to be made about this transcendent setting and special friend kind of friendship. When I began the work in these neighborhoods eight years ago, I believed that to gain the confidence of these families, and to be certain that what we experienced was "valid," the settings and relationships had to put us all at ease. Any cue that reminded us of my own participating observation would render all responses stilted, self-conscious, invalid. Patronizing actions, undue cordiality or ingratiation necessarily implied failure in friendship, failure in investigation, failure in science.

After eight years I have turned these beliefs around. My periodic stumbling ways and ungainly silences, along with William D.'s and Adrien's occasional formalities and so-called best behaviorisms, symbolize our collective desire to create that transcendent situation of mutual recognition. For within it lies the care that each of us has for one another, a care that derives in part from the awareness that our relationship is to some extent unnatural, even contrived. Still, the act of contriving a role or presence can be a creative act, one of giving and of increased consciousness of self. It can be an offering.

Surely Mrs. Williams, with whom my friendship is brittle and unsettled, realizes that I have more knowledge on certain topics than I may share with her at a given time. But I know that she has knowledge and feelings that she keeps out of my sight as well. Sadly, our culture continually assesses the differences between us and the materials we share and keep from one another in terms of equalities and inequalities. And at this point in our historical development, we are led to believe that I have "more" knowledge and that she has "more" feelings.

This matter of inequalities too, enters our friendship and causes us to be self-conscious and on guard. Both of us are aware of those who are suspicious of the fact that at times I can find nothing to say to her or to the children, or that I might be overcome by feelings, even childlike feelings. We are aware too, of those who chastise her for restraining herself with me, or perhaps for merely allowing me to enter her home. As best we can, therefore, we play out political roles — the politics, that is, of our experiences together — hoping to combat the asymmetries produced by the culture, the society, our age, sex, race, and social standing, and by the rights and privileges that put me at an advantage in doing this type of work.

There is little, then, about this form of research that allows for so-called objective inquiry. Even if I chose to assume the role of indifferent observer, as if that role yielded objectivity, I know that William D., Adrien, and their parents would never let it pass; not after all these years. Invariably they remark on those days when I appear more disheveled than usual, just as they remark on those instances when I fail to tell them of feelings my face and body are already emitting. Upon hearing their remarks, I am reminded of the subjective nature of the inquiry, and that what I observe and record is not only material experienced by me, it is in part generated by me. I often think that the few aspects of William D.'s and Adrien's lives that I might record with some modicum of objectivity are the very aspects I never directly confront. Yet even these aspects would receive subjective responses, responses that are in no way inferior to the knowledge gained through so-called objective assessments.

In the end, the research builds upon encounters with human beings who by nature act egoistically. The encounters are themselves processes of mutual inquiry, observation, and expression; explication and understanding lie in the encounter. The emphasis rests on the single case, and the growing series of single involvements. A genuine encounter precludes comparison and assessment. To assess these families, in effect, is to transcend them and thereby negate the mutuality of recognition and the politics of equality. The self-consciousness, finally, born in these encounters connotes both wariness and self-awareness, precursors, clearly, of human conscience and tolerance.

What these children from a poor neighborhood know of and feel about politics, and what they may be willing to tell a rich, white, "formally" educated male sociologist constitute a major methodological issue. Another issue is the degree to which these children are committed to the political system that underwrites portions of the culture to which they have at best minimal access. Given these two orientations, a subjective methodology and the political realities facing these children, I cannot see how anyone can manage his temper and, in the face of it all, remain sanguine. Granted, subjective efforts require a constant check on one's perceptions and feelings. The first rule, we recall, is to pay attention to what the person before us is saying and to what has been evoked in ourselves. But beyond this attention to the mutuality of the relationship, if unadulterated, barely controllable anger fails to accompany the lack of human rights, then I think that the words of these families have not been heard and felt as they ultimately must be felt. The words may be analyzed, used for some ulterior purpose, or passed on to those who are "supposed" to hear them, but they have not been felt, and the response to them has not been forthcoming.

This is not to say that one always finds the appropriate response to another person's anger. I think, for example, of a summer afternoon when Mrs. Williams expressed her anger about the government and I could find no way to reply to her:

"It's the government that goes ruining my family, no one else. It's the government that goes messing up. I can't afford these prices. You see how they raise them on us every month. I can't fix up my house like those rich ladies. I can't even travel on the bus anymore and feel safe. You think anybody cares whether the children just might be too hot out there? Or whether they might be too cold in here when the winter comes? You think anybody cares whether some guy decides to raise the rent and give us nothing for it? There isn't anybody in the government who cares. I can't get anybody to listen to us. What the hell do they think we're asking for anyway, a million dollars? All we want is a stoplight on the corner of Gloucester and Saint Marks. All we want is for prices to be fair. That's all. So what do we get? We get all these people coming around wanting to know if we're cheating on welfare. Checking all around looking for my husband. We don't want welfare, but what do they expect us to eat on or live on if the government doesn't help us find jobs?

"The first thing they do is let our schools go to hell, then they tell us we aren't educated enough to do anything constructive. Then they arrange it so we can't use the hospitals and clinics, and then they tell us we're sick too often. They take all the jobs away and give them to rich folks or college students, and then they tell us that we're lazy, that we don't want to work, that we're cheating on welfare. They move us out so they can build some superhighway that only businessmen use coming in every day from the suburbs, and then they tell us we have no right to complain about our neighborhood. That's what the government gives me. Pain. Pain's what I get, along with a bunch of promises every four years so I'll go out and vote for someone. And even if I want to vote they can find all kinds of reasons why I can't. That's what the government gives me."

Anger and outrage cannot ultimately shape the intellectual and legislative processes required in the determination of human rights. Yet, when anger never appears, when day-to-day heartache and anguish, and personal responses to them, are deemed inappropriate for intellectuals, researchers, and legislators, then that transcendent situation of mutual recognition, as subjective as it must be, is never approached, and the traditional distances and inequalities between people are reiterated and affirmed. Then, too, institutions and government need never change, and the words of Adrien Keller and William D. Williams remain charming, even precocious, but not legitimate influences of personal consciousness or social change, nor testimonies of the need for political and economic enfranchisement.

Here may be the crucial point of separation between myself and the families about whom this book has been written. I have no doubt that the children, as we say, "opened up" with me and shared personal and tender experiences as well as some hurtful ones. I have no doubt that they care for me. I want to say that we love one another. We also hold back things and recognize that certain issues, and the emotions connected to them, are better left unsaid. One such issue is that I can leave them there, in their inadequately heated homes, with a meager amount of food ready to be placed on the table, and return to my own home, my own race, my own social position and cultural securities.

Occasionally I speak about this fact with Adrien and William D. While we mention the differences between us, we never pursue these differences in the same way and with the same urgency as we pursue topics like food prices or urban crime. Perhaps this is because we recognize the possibility of our separating from one another once these differences are articulated and countenanced; and this eventuality I, for one, want to avoid. While we are clearly not all the other has, our friendship, as lopsided as status, age, race, sex, and purpose of research render it, is valuable and, at this moment in our lives, needed. The children say this in more subtle ways when they remind me of our meeting time for the following week. They say it explicitly too. Several months before the elections, William D. told me:

"I'm already looking ahead to when the elections are over. Then we'll have lots of other things to talk about. But what I wonder about with you is whether you'll want to talk to me and the kids around here anymore after that. Nate Thayer said you may be going away."

"Not true, William D."

"Well, he said you might be going, leaving Boston and all, and, man, as white as you are, I wouldn't like that. Seems to me that the way we should work it out is that when I get a little older I probably won't want to be seeing you that much. Then I can go, and you can find boys who are my age now, you know, maybe they're eight or nine now, and do with them like you're doing with Adrien and me. But that ain't going to be for a couple more years the way I see it."

Many factors kindle the possibility of our separating, not the least of which is maturation and the logical tenure of friendships made at specific times for specific reasons. Another factor is that one of anger again. Whereas right from the beginning I felt angry about the state of affairs, the state of politics and knowledge that yields such unjust realities, I didn't hear a commensurate amount of anger in the families. Tendrils of anger pushed their way into our conversations, but the explosive fury that I often felt was not evidenced by them.

Once I was tempted to suggest that these families are beyond feeling this anger, this fury of constant heartache. Or maybe the anger was displaced onto other people and other issues. Or perhaps it was pride that silenced it, or it was beaten out of them over the years. As time went on, however, the anger came forward, though with the children it rarely surfaced with the force I am certain they were feeling. On some occasions, as with William D. one after-noon, the anger was more safely expressed in a story of someone else's hurts and feeling of betrayal, although even then William D. was frightened by it.

We were walking home from his school when he told me of being with a group of boys who were planning to attack a high school teacher. The teacher, apparently, had been play-ing basketball with some older students when a group of younger boys begged him to let them take some shots from the sidelines. For an instant it seemed as if the teacher would consent, but as he was about to throw the ball to Billy Romey Deangelo, one of William D.'s friends, he flipped the ball behind himself instead. The older boys on the court were impressed by the teacher's trickery. They yelled, "Hey, hey, what do you say, Walt Frazier," and "Give one big assist to the Jo Jo," meaning Jo Jo White of the Boston Celtics. But Romey Deangelo was furious. He had held his hands out for the ball, reaching over the out-of-bounds line expect-ing the ball to be passed to him. When it wasn't, he held his hands forward for a last instant almost prayerfully, then let them fall.

"Stupid son of a bitch motherfuck," he muttered. "Gonna break your ass for that trick."

Later that day, according to William D., Romey got a group together behind the firehouse on Plymouth Street. Several boys wanted to report the teacher to a principal, or at least talk it out with him before taking action, but Romey refused. Talking wasn't good enough.

Three days later Romey and several boys jumped the teacher as he was getting into his car. A second group of students, however, came to the teacher's rescue and Romey's group surrendered. Then all the boys went back together into the school with the teacher and had a long talk.

William D. did not attend this meeting; nor did he witness the aborted attack. He did report that Romey felt humiliated and claimed that someone had tipped off the teacher. It was not by accident, Romey said, that these other boys were there just when they were needed. William D. never questioned Romey's assertion, and I never questioned William D. any further on this incident.

Adrien and William D. hold back anger from me partly because for them I am, along with others, a symbol of the very culture that constrains them. Pressure is put on them to stop talking with white people, and I understand this, just as pressure is put on me to terminate my relationships with them and their families. All of this must be acknowledged, for as I have said much of this story of children and politics lies in my friendships with Adrien and William D. More than just what they say or I say, it is the encounter, the two cultures coming together to yield words, ideas, and passions, that predominates. Our behavior together, coupled with the respective evolution of our peoples, keeps their anger out of sight — not out of hearing distance, but out of sight. And so our friendships are safeguarded, at least for the time being.

Nothing, then, is more troublesome than to leave the Williamses and Kellers realizing how much empty space remains between them and me, and that all of us are aware of this space. They can see the space and outline its parameters. How often during the ride home from their neighborhood do I hear the advice of well-meaning parents to their children: "You will be meeting Mrs. Jones this afternoon, son. She is different from us because she is black. But you mustn't say anything about this to her face. Okay? Promise me you won't." The space that separates me from the Williamses and Kellers is filled with the faces of children. They are open faces, in my fantasy, open to hope, to knowledge and opportunity. They are knowing faces as well, capable of expressions of wonderment and betrayal, thankfulness and cynicism. They are also wise faces, and this part of my fantasy is not derived from overromanticizing them, but from knowing them.

Children of poverty, like children of any group destined to be kept from the center of the society and hence from its protective rights and shelters, learn the language and value systems of two cultures, their own and the culture that withholds from them. These children in our country — economically deprived as they are, but who speak two languages: Spanish *and* English, Portuguese *and* English, Italian *and* English, Yiddish *and* English, or one of numerous native American languages *and* English — represent the complex and rich inheritance which is theirs. Despite the presence of these children, there is an unrelenting urge to see them and their families as special cases or categorical types and impute a natural ignorance to them, probably because the imputation justifies the disenfranchisement. At times this process seems less hurtful because we can say, Well, they are only children and they will learn. You will see, in time we will "bring them up" to our level.

The imputation however, is inaccurate and dangerous. I confess I began with the idea of sampling children from various economic levels of society — what we ordinarily conceive of as the lower, middle, and upper classes — so that a genuine comparison of children's political attitudes and sophistication might be achieved. This plan made sociological sense, as many studies would indicate. Yet as I began to write, I realized that comparison took away from a central point: young black persons raised in urban poverty know and care about the very political system that affects not only their own lives, but the lives of people whose communities but a few miles away they may never see. It is essential, therefore, that at certain times we speak about these young persons and their families and nothing more, and refrain from comparing them with their age counterparts someplace else, or even with other children in their own neighborhood. For in the comparison process we can too easily lose an appreciation for the single child who stands before us, the knowledge and feelings of that child, and the glory that must be that single child's history and future. While clearly a useful and valid method of research, the comparison process can also further, albeit unintentionally, the very standards and criteria that lead to such assessments as "disadvantagedness," and "inferior performance and intelligence."

Conc The goal, therefore, is not to study poor black children for the purpose of constructing behavioral criteria to be used later with rich white children — a black IQ test, as it were. The goal is to establish and preserve human rights, rights sanctified by law, culture, and psychology, that honor human beings and safeguard the time during which they walk upon the earth, especially as children.

Under any political system that evolves in a truly equitable society, individuals will continue to need help of one sort or another. They will be in pain or feel despair, they will seek advice on how to read faster, or perhaps how to raise their children or grow their produce. Their requests, however, in this equitable society will be interpreted as acts of strength, not as ineptitude. At present, the overriding message of those who periodically dip into poor communities as if testing icy water with their toes is that the people of America's inner cities are weak, ignorant, primitive, filled with "raw" capacities, and unwilling to "help their own cause." These reports then make their way into the minds of America's citizens, and into their abiding legislation, newspapers, and textbooks. The result is captured in my own surprise several years ago when I simply had to acknowledge how splendid are the minds of the young people I was meeting in communities like Roxbury, Dorchester, Somerville, and Roslindale. It is captured, too, in my own blind spots, my patronizing gestures, and my inability at times to transcend a proper role or agreed-upon expectation, and in those encounters listen to what was being said to me, about me, and within me.

When I first began this work, I ran from the accounts of people like the Williamses and Kellers. I pushed them away through my sociological expertise or so-called clinical insightfulness. Even when I listened in the "right" and "open" manner, I distanced myself from these "subjects" by taking myself out of the writing altogether so that no one would be reminded that I had been with them, and been touched by them. In the name of objective social science and proper psychological and political demeanor, no one should know how I felt about them.

Later, I made an equally imprudent mistake when I came to believe that little in sociology or psychology seemed pertinent to my discussions with the children and their families. In fact it was the people themselves who encouraged me to call upon sociological and clinical perspectives just as they were doing. I think, in this light, of the day when, in describing some predicament, Adrien remarked:

"Well, you know how it is. The family without a father turns to its oldest children. They sort of expect that the oldest boy will have to be getting a job pretty soon like his father, if his father was still alive, and that the oldest girl will start helping in the house, like being an assistant to her mother. It's like they have in schools, you know, when the teacher's absent and someone has to substitute for her in class. A substitute, that's me. I guess I'm the substitute mother in our family, and my brother Quintin and my mother, since they're really the only ones working, are like substitute fathers. This way, you see, it's like our family really hasn't changed all that much, except that we miss our father. All the work we do to keep the family going isn't about to change that. It seems funny to me though," she added with a smile, "that we only say that my mother and brother are working, 'cause it sure seems like I'm working too, at school and at home in the kitchen. Maybe that's because they get paid for their work and I don't. Hey, maybe I should get paid too. I shouldn't say that though, should I?"

Also in the beginning, I confess to wondering whether two people would be "enough" for this study, and whether the absence of abstract interpretation and analysis of the children's attitudes would cause others to feel that something vital was missing. As much as the practice of psychotherapy at times demands interpretations of language and behavior, in this different sort of enterprise, I believe that people's words stand on their own and that often an overriding analysis is uncalled-for, if not an outright impertinence. The reader must remember that my arrangement with these families does not imply psychological treatment or analysis, but rather reporting and describing, or just plain paying attention.

Analysis of social, political, and psychological phenomena, an inevitable operation in a society dominated by technological rationality, is often useful and enlightening. But analysis can also mean the distancing of people, the gratuitous "upgrading" of human groups. It can lead to a belief that in order to speak for oneself and one's people, one has to learn the appropriate "mother tongue," or the language and rhetoric of vocal and powerful leaders. Analysis implies that the words of someone, a resident of some community, a farmer, a patient in psychoanalysis, are by themselves incomplete bits of data waiting maturation. What makes them "complete" is the analysis: rational explanation; their systematic placement not just in a particular context or series of categories — for these operations we all undertake in listening to speech — but in some higher order and abstracted level of comprehension. For the present work, analysis would mean not only making something of William D.'s and Adrien's words, but using their words to develop an overarching statement, a theory of the self in contemporary society.

Without doubt, the task of rendering everyday reality into conceptualizations and explanatory theories is a formidable one, and one essential for understanding our single lives and our cultures, as well as for the development of intellectual discourse. Yet the generation of social science theory and the act of abstracting human expression to achieve levels of more comprehensive awareness are not the goals of this research. These are not the reasons I came to know these families, nor the reasons for writing about these two children. Interpretation and analysis nonetheless remain a part of this enterprise. They are, however, performed implicitly. In the selection of the material, in the inevitable editing of dialogues and personal reflections and reactions, rest interpretation, theory, conceptualization, and, just as important, the moments of polemics and moralizing.

As is true with most types of theory building and interpretation in the social sciences, this implicit, almost playwright form of interpretation carries its own brand of prejudgments and abiding perspectives. They are unavoidable. In making interpretations and analyses in the form of experiencing, selecting, and ordering, one hopes that the truth is accurately described and that the ethic of enhancing life is never lost; but one can never be certain. Pure abstract analysis, like the structured interview, often masks the uncertainties and vagaries of the reality from which the analyst can never be extricated — unless, of course, the analyst never encounters the reality chosen for analysis. It was this point I tried to make earlier when I said that I might have a more objective grasp of those phases of William D.'s and Adrien's lives where I play no part. But when one does play a part, when one is implicated in the lives of those one observes or "studies," then abstract analysis becomes a more difficult psychological and intellectual chore. Distancing oneself becomes an impossible strategy, an implausible experience, and using these people's words as grist for one's intellectual machinery becomes an ugly, if not incongruous undertaking. When, finally, I go back and analyze, in the typical sense, I negate the encounters and deny the truths of the subjective inquiry.

In this context, I understand but am saddened nevertheless by two expressions I often hear made in connection with this kind of work. The first goes something like "It's good that you're going out there to those homes, talking with those families, and having their dirt rub off on you." Strangely, it is rarely suggested that one might be cleansed in his contact with the poor, the obscure, the disenfranchised. Fearing the charge of sentimentality or overromanticizing, I rarely say publicly that I have felt cleansed by these families, but I feel it. Not on every visit, but I often feel it, and suspect the families know when this eerie religious moment has come and gone.

Apart from whether one is dirtied or cleansed, does this expression mean that one is in some way made less a person because of his association with children or with poverty? Is one now half a man because so many of his hours are spent associating with children in ways we normally characterize as being feminine? Does the fact that women engage in the care of children more than men influence our perceptions of children generally, and of those men who enter into friendships with children and their families, and become in small measure a part of their lives? If, because of a subjective posture, one becomes half a man, then indeed he is a child, expressive rather than analytic, filled with sentiment, and catering to unrealizable dreams and ambitions — all of which suggest he is not yet ready to be taken seriously. He often bumbles, sits in silence, has outbreaks of temper, generally "overidentifies" with those he visits, and in no way resembles the image we maintain of a scholar or scientist.

The second expression goes "I don't know what to do with the words of these children or their parents; what to make of them, what to think about them." The statement reminds me of my own reactions to concerts where I feel an uneasy urge to wait for the following morning's review before deciding whether I liked what I heard. Undoubtedly, analysis enhances one's appreciation of music, in the present context the words of children. It must never detract, however, from one's ability to hear and pay attention, or minimize one's belief in one's capacity to hear, appreciate, and respond. While analysis, be it explicit or implicit, aids in understanding and offers the possibility of enlarging the sensuous experience, it can also be a self-imposed inhibitor of the feelings evoked by the experience — a constraint, in other words, on reaction.

Similarly, the structured interview in which prepared questions are arranged in careful order, while yielding valuable information, purposely acts as a constraint on personal reaction. In a sense, the structured interview becomes a barrier between people, albeit a porous one, as well as a means of keeping responses of all kinds under control. Whereas the content yielded through the structured interview is unpredictable, the interaction describing the interview is more or less prearranged. This is not to say that so-called free-form interviews, what we have called "encounters," are free of restraints on behavior and feeling. As we have seen, they are not. Indeed the presence of these restraints may be the basis of the tension one experiences in becoming implicated, if only by reading, in the lives of other persons, particularly those with whom one rarely associates.

The tension, then, is between structuring and analyzing material and remaining vulnerable to whatever has been evoked by this material, without utilizing techniques to control and shape it. It is not merely a tension caused by a competition between intellectual and emotional resources. Rather, the tension is caused partly by the political, economic, and educational disparities in our culture, and partly too by our social roles and positions, our stations in life, and our learned beliefs of what is appropriate and inappropriate behavior for ourselves, for those richer and more powerful than we, and for those poorer and less powerful than we.

It is a tension caused, moreover, by those we feel to be transgressing in some ways, those who seem capricious in their manner, and somehow improperly respectful of style, custom, and protocol. Analysis may be a means of combating these transgressors, these persons who travel where they are not meant to travel, work where they are not meant to work, commune with those with whom they are not meant to commune, and subjectively experience what they ought to be objectively describing and assessing. It may also be a means of counteracting the feeling that we have been intruded on; that our feelings, in other words, have been accidentally ignited. Abstract, depersonalized analysis, then, is an essential intellectual and creative act that expands learning. It is also an encumbrance; a blockade to feeling and human contact; a filibuster to quintessential human expression and exchange.

I have dwelled on these points because they seem especially relevant to a work devoted to children and politics. Do we, after all, give credence to the expressions of children, or do we make their words into something else? Do we listen to children when they announce their ideas in "children's ways," but turn away from their responses to our adult culture? Do we place full faith in the proposals and philosophies advanced by those whose language seems somehow "immature," grammatically incorrect, piquant or charming, but ultimately "naive" and "unskilled"? The sounds of language, along with its cognitive, cultural, and psychological roots, emerge as a fundamental political reality, just as the traditionally defined verbal aptitude remains a key to achievement. If people do not sound exactly "right," if when they speak we conjure up foreign images and foreign matter, then those persons will be derogated or, conversely, found to be excessively delightful and amusing.

It is evident that social scientists disagree on their assessments of ghetto children's language. Some call it a form characteristically different from, but no "better" or worse than, the form of upper-middle-class white children. Others suggest that the language patterns of poor black children are inferior in some ways to the language patterns of upper-middle-class children. In the political context, "improper" speech is associated with sounding like and therefore reflecting the intelligence of a child. And if one sounds like a child, then he or she tends to be discredited, for how can a child contribute significantly to society and to politics except by staying in school and steering clear of trouble? Gradually, language differences and the sense of foreignness these differences evoke in us serve to make permanent the separations we are already feeling. The separations, further-more, are translated into superior and inferior status — the intelligent and the ignorant, the adults and the children.

It is for these reasons that I felt it necessary to include not merely quotations from William D. and Adrien, but ex-tended samples of our conversations. A snippet of speech is not unlike a photograph, or what we occasionally believe a photograph to be. Both are used as illustration or counter-point to "more serious" art forms. Books are spiced with photographs or fragments of speech from eleven-year-old children to encourage the reader's imagination or break the monotony of expository writing. This usage, however, de-grades both children's language and photography as it denies them the potential of being autonomous artistic expressions.

The story of the Williams and Keller families is not in-tended as illustration of or data for some "greater" and more mature product. The words are what I have tried to convey; their words to me, mine to them, and finally that mixture of all our words together. Over time, we have become friends, although in the beginning, as I have said, I was reluctant to have this happen. I looked at the children strictly as illus-trations of some "problem," "phenomenon," or "condition." In addition, I was "ghettoizing" everything until the chil-dren became little more than neighborhood informants, rep-resentatives of poverty, poignant objects that I could hold up to make a case for their intelligence, political sophistica-tion, and need for legal rights. As long as I used fragments of speech and worried about what their words meant, the children remained newspaper photographs, postcards, some-*thing* to regard as illustration but not people to be taken seriously in and of themselves.

Much of this has changed — at least my intentions and behavior with these children have changed. Probably, too, the content of what I have heard and seen has changed. And more recently, still another development has taken place.

Throughout the year prior to the elections, as political talk with Adrien and William D. became more intense, I carried a dream of writing several volumes on children. Perhaps these volumes would be limited to political and economic issues, perhaps not, but children's lives would be the source of these books. Soon after the elections, however, my interests suddenly shifted away from children and all their activities. I felt not unlike I imagine pediatricians must feel at some stage in their work, wanting to move into other specialities where children's hurts need not be confronted every day. Old people, I decided, those who seem to be farthest from children and childhood, would be an ideal group to study. They aren't, of course, separated from childhood any more than the rest of us, but perhaps their appearance and environment would allow me to forget the children. Or perhaps I could study men my own age. Surely they would lead me away from the children in Roxbury.

This desire to switch careers as a way of warding off certain emotions or silencing personal upheavals is something many of us experience. Most of us, however, the pediatricians included, fortunately stay at it, gathering together new hopes and old resignations and resisting the impulse to abandon something or someone. The accusation leveled at us during these momentary periods of doubts is that we "work out" our identities through the lives of those we interview, teach, or simply observe. While the accusation is cryptic, and the use of the word "identity" not sufficiently comprehensive, the import of the accusation contains a truth. Decisions to remain on the job, to stay with children, may well affect one's identity. But any decision may influence the continuity of the self over time and the sense of inner sameness that are, theoretically, foundations of identity. Confronting a child, or anyone for that matter, necessarily affects our sense of personal evolution and commitment and touches the chords of our identity. Confrontations, implying as they do mutual acknowledgment of persons, must influence our sense of identity for they cause us to become reacquainted with ourselves.

The accusation of working out one's identity with children is extremely serious if truths are distorted and identity formation found to be the reason for engaging children in the first place. But these potential dangers hold true in any human contact, be it with an employer or colleague, parent or friend. For any encounter may cause someone to feel that his or her identity has been affirmed, or put somehow into jeopardy. And that this happens is not necessarily a sign that one is "insecure," but rather that the capacity to become reacquainted with one's history and imagined destiny endures.

Still, when the work involves children, the question of "identity seeking" is frequently heard, probably because we believe that those who study, teach, or treat children have never completely resolved the childlike components of their own identity. While this remains a matter for psychiatrists and psychohistorians to decide, unless of course children begin to publish their investigations of us, one takes from this "identity seeking" accusation the contention that possessing childlike components in one's adult identity is pathological — and this fact has serious implications for our fundamental perceptions of ourselves and our children.

Now, why such a discussion at the conclusion of this book? The political worlds of children, the insurance money that has never been granted, rising food prices, the lead content of paint, steep rents, inadequate plumbing, and insufficient amounts of food have special meaning for this brand of research. I too can be accused of exploiting these children, using them to further my own career if not increase the legitimacy of a research method. Perhaps I do exploit them, for there is a degree of exploitation in anything resembling what we label a "case study," a term that causes disquiet in me. I hope, however, that by allowing the reader to meet these children, to experience some of my ruminations in their presence, and to listen to these long passages of conversation, the children will not be viewed as mere illustrations or one-dimensional "subjects" alive on this earth to further causes that ultimately will not benefit them.

Perhaps the work helps to confirm the findings of other investigators. Perhaps, too, enterprises of this sort give these young people a presence, and eventually full human stature, particularly in communities where their voices may never be heard. In a sense, this might constitute a small portion of what their own vote might look like. But observe that throughout their accounts and expressions, and certainly in their dreams, these young people speak only for themselves. Rarely do they recount the ways of *all* children. Their approach is personalized and carefully delineated. They take seriously the slogan "One person, one vote" and speak accordingly. Their accounts tell us, in part, how their lives are led; our reactions to these accounts tell them what we have heard, and how we have heard it.

As I reach the end, I again feel compelled to raise the issue of these young people's controlled outrage at certain political realities. No doubt my own make-up causes me to hunt for outrage or anger in others. No doubt, too, the more anger, or any emotion, for that matter, that might appear in a book, political speech, or simple conversation, the more the writer or speaker is accused of immaturity or childishness. To scream, swear, or appear overly impassioned is taken as an indication that the tissue of childhood has not yet been covered over. So much of what we normally consider political socialization involves teaching people to control their impulses and feelings, and to behave properly — which means like adults. Retaliation and righteous indignation, the raw display of temper, and, on a collective level, demonstrations of violence "prove" that childhood, with its muscular and emotional uncoordination, outright animalism, and lack of human respect, predominates.

Both Adrien and William D. are capable of great quantities of love, some of which I have received. For the moment, however, I have not received the anger I know their friends and families at times receive. I am not eager, naturally, to receive their anger, yet I feel that if in some genuine way I could have it out with them so that in the end we would see that we had survived and were still able to call upon that love, some of the space between us might be reduced.

In this regard, I was struck several weeks ago watching a teacher permit two boys, eight or nine years old, one black, one white, to fight each other in a school yard. At the conclusion of the fight, with no one hurt but with feelings surely dented a trifle, the boys discovered they had remained friends, if not better friends. They learned, first, that the expression of anger did not destroy their caring for one another and, second, that the school yard situation with the teacher present rendered their combat safe. In four or five years — for America will not change sufficiently in this time — that same fight will be construed as a racial conflict and will, most probably, produce serious implications for their school and community.

I am left, then, with this irony of reuniting people in part through anger. It is an ending I did not foresee and one which suggests that I have not adequately pursued this one emotion with the children. Or maybe the time for this pursuit is not quite right. Nonetheless, the separation between us, the space that like a receptacle receives my blind spots and patronizing gestures, as well as their feelings of attachment, "identification," ambivalence, or just plain caring, is a space of politics. It is where the politics begins and ends, where disenfranchisement, oppression, and colonialization breed, and where research of the sort I have reported takes place. Words, intellects, and emotions live in this space, as do laws, customs, history, and scholarship. Each word we speak constitutes a molecular tension, relative quiescence followed by frenzied action of human relationships. This in essence is the space of my encounters with these children, their families and neighbors; it is the site of the distillates of America's political system in this one moment, and in this one context. And while I leave it with no strong feelings of hope, I am able to call upon moments of encouragement and satisfaction:

"You're doing the best you can," Mrs. Keller assured me one day not long after Adrien's reaction to the food boycott. "And so are the children. Some of the problems, you know, can't be treated so easily. I know, we share them; you forget that. I've got the same problems you have talking to these ten- and eleven-year-old big shots I got running around my house. Stubborn? Ooo-eee, can they ever be stubborn, and sassy. They got mouths on them, sometimes I can't believe my ears. If they talked like this at school I bet someone for sure would hit them right across their mouths.

"But you've seen now," she went on, "that they also have a whole lot of wisdom in them. If anybody gives them the chance they're going to tell them a whole lot. What I'm hoping you'll tell me, though, when you get through with all your work, is just where they get this wisdom from. They sure don't get it from me 'cause I don't know half the things they're talking about most of the time, especially when they've just come back from their school. It must be the teachers who put all these ideas and politics in their heads. That and the television maybe, although most of the time all I see them watching is cartoons. I suppose maybe God gives it to them. He gives them the wisdom when He gives them their strength."

"And they sure have strength," I echoed her thought.

"You can say that again. Wise, strong, that's the way He makes them. I guess that's what He figures a person needs to get through the little bit of living we're meant to do. But you see, Tom, here's where you and I aren't exactly what you'd call similar. God gives each of us a small amount of time. To some He gives a little more, to some a little less." She glanced at the photograph of her husband. "You remember what I've told you. But that's not the whole point to it. The real point, you see, is that to some groups of people He gives a whole lot of space to move around in, to explore, to grow and become something that makes them happy, and maybe makes their parents a little happier too, 'cause that's important. There isn't a parent in the world who doesn't care what happens to her child. But happy or not, you folks all got big spaces to move around in, to feel yourself in, and make it fine in the world, just like all of us in the Keller family believe you are.

"My children, though, they have a very little space given to them by the Lord. Barely big enough. It's sort of like

handing down clothes from one child to the next when you
have children real close in age. The minute one child can't
fit into this little pair of pants, you pass them on real quick
to the next child 'cause there's only a small bit of time when
they'll be fitting that second child. See what I mean?
They're already worn, and like that space I was telling you
about, they're barely big enough for him. He barely fits in
them. Everything's this way where we live. Everything.
Barely enough room in this house, barely enough food for
Adrien to fix for her meals. Even when I don't eat as much
as I'd like, there's barely enough. And *my* children, don't
forget, have it a whole lot better than most children. And
there's barely enough room for them in the streets, and up
on the roofs, and in their schools, barely enough places for
them to play, barely enough money for them to buy what
they need, and certainly nothing left over if they'd like to go
out and have a good time once in a while with their friends.
I'm tough on them when they ask, but I sure would like to
have it to give to them. But I can't, so I have to protect myself and my own feelings, my pride, don't you see, and convince them that they really don't need to go buy anything
and that we already have everything we need; everything
He intended for us to have." She looked quickly above her.

"But now, like I was saying, my children don't have
enough of that space that your children are going to have au-
tomatic like, because of you and your wife. Now, don't go
misunderstanding me," she added quickly. "I'm not just
talking about not being able to travel and see all the holy
things one ought to be seeing on the earth before one dies,
although that would be awfully nice. What I'm talking
about is a very special meaning of space. It all comes to one
thing: Nobody, at least nobody that I can see, and certainly
no politician fellow, really wants us to have our children.

That's the size of it." She was nodding as though her argument was at last formed. "They don't want these children around here. Fact is, they as much as tell us this in their way. First they go making all sorts of rules and laws about welfare. Then they come back to us with ideas about contraception, birth control measures, you know, all kinds of talk about cutting down the size of our families. Don't get me wrong. I believe in all this. I don't want families growing bigger and bigger just for the sake of, you know, growing bigger." She grinned and held her hand over her stomach to signify the shape of pregnancy. "But outside of the accidents these little ones are having now and then, folks around here want their children. It isn't all we want, like you read about us sometimes in the papers, but we want them. Cut them out from us and you cut life out from us. Take our children away and you've taken away most of that little bitty space that belongs to us. It was never much to begin with, but it *is* something, and children are a very important part of it.

"But the politicians, they don't want these children. So why not? Why don't they want us having children? You ever ask yourself that question? Huh?" I remained still. "Well, I'll tell you. Because we're a burden to them is why. We're a burden to this country and all those men who make the rules we have to live by every day of our lives. What they'd really like is to get rid of us. Yessir. Every one of us. Children, parents, grandparents, every last one of us. All our families, here and everywhere. They'd probably try it too, except some good people might get in their way."

"You thinking about genocide, Mrs. Keller?"

"I don't know what the word is they got for it, but I'm telling you there isn't a mother in this neighborhood doesn't know, doesn't feel in here" — she lay her hand on her bosom — "that people in this country don't want *our* children no more. It's a very simple idea they've got in their heads. You get rid of the children and soon enough you'll get rid of all the other people too right after them. No children today, no parents tomorrow, no more anybody in these communities to annoy them. Then they could go pulling all these buildings down and build their kinds of buildings so their kind of people could have even *more* space than they already got, which is more than they need. Now, Tom, you going to tell me you really need more space? You want to tell me that? I don't think so. Seems to me from just watching you move in and out of here every week that you already got more space than you can use.

"But you see, the reason I'm glad to have you coming around here, no matter why you do, is because when you talk with Adrien and the other children, I know that for those minutes, for those small minutes, you just might be giving them some of that extra space of yours. Maybe you don't even know you're doing it, but I can tell. I can tell from what they say, not just about you but about a whole lot of things. They're moving around a little more, talking about things maybe no one talked to them about before, like their teachers will do. It's the same thing. Now don't you go thinking I'm letting you come by so's the children can go believing you're their pretend father. I'm not thinking that for a minute. It's just that they got to know where you come from, and where your wife and children come from, otherwise they might be stuck where they are, and where I *know* those politician fellows want them to be. Right here!

"But when I see them talking with you and their teachers and some of the other folks who come by, I always have the same thought crossing my mind. You can use my children, like we talked about that one time, and put what they say in your books. But you have to use them in another way too, and that's just to know them, and learn from them, and worry about what's going to become of them. My worrying and doing isn't ever going to be enough, 'cause I'm their mother, and that puts me in the same space with them. But when you go worrying about my children, and the little Williams boy, and some of these other children, then I'll feel better knowing that people like you won't let these politicians try to get rid of them. Those people in Washington and the State House here have to know that even if we don't have enough money to fight them on all these issues and all these laws they make for us, at least they'll have to take on your kind, the kind who God gives the big spaces to.

"Now, I got another thought while we're talking about this."

"Please." We both moved with a bit of discomfort in our chairs.

"I want you to know something about what *I* think politics means. Not a whole lot, mind you, 'cause I know it's the children you're really interested in, which is all right and the way it should be. They come first. But *my* political beliefs may be different from yours. I can't see that anything's going to happen if we keep going like we have been. All this anger everyone's carrying around is getting us nowhere. Oh, they make a little change over here, and then another little one over there" — she extended her arm and swirled her hand as though stirring liquid in a cup — "but nothing all that much is changing. One President comes, another President goes, but prices go up and up and still there's no jobs. That's what changes," she exclaimed, "things get worse!

"So now I have to ask myself just what should we do, and try as I might I can't see nothing short of a real revolution changing this country. No matter what they do with what they got now, rich folks are still rich folks, and poor folks are still poor folks. So, it seems to me that since they've just about tried everything else but revolution, that's going to have to be what they do next, which leads me to what you might call my dilemma.

"Politicians, like I said, don't want the children. They want to do them in so they don't have to deal with poor folks anymore. We can't go on much longer this way, if we have any brains left, which we do, even folks like me who quit school before I should have. But I can't feel right about telling this to my children just yet. They're too young to be getting it, to really be understanding what a revolution's all about. So I wait, and in the meantime I think that the very best that can happen is for them to be in their schools, and maybe talking with you and their teachers about whatever you all talk about together. But when do I talk to them about *my* ideas? That's my question. When's the right time? Now? Do I talk to them now? Do I talk to them later on sometime? And if I wait, will I be doing what my parents did to me, and their parents did to them? Will I be waiting too long? Will we be hurting these children more by telling them, or waiting for just a bit more time? That's my dilemma, don't you see. That's the question I have. How do I work it out so they have the money they need and the clothes and food and doctors, and anything else they'll want while they're growing up, and protect them, but not so much that they don't know what's really going on, and what's going to have to happen?

"They don't know now. I can tell you that. Quintin maybe does, but the others don't know. They can't see their future coming up over the hill like I can. I know, though; I've been through it. I've seen the politicians and the business people. I know their type. I've seen babies born and all sorts of people die. I've buried a husband. No sir, the children don't have *all* the wisdom. They don't have *all* the understanding of politics that you need growing up in this country today. But God bless them, they have the strength. That's one thing they have for sure. Thank the Lord they don't feel the weariness I feel. But see, even with all that strength, they can't help me with my dilemma. And come to think of it" — she leaned forward in the chair — "if you're so interested in children and their political ways and attitudes, I should think you might want to concentrate a good deal about that dilemma of mine, until, well, until it becomes your dilemma too. What do you say to that?"

"I say I believe you're right. It is a dilemma for all of us."

"Well then, I say God bless the children, and God bless us weary old adults too."

References

Aberbach, Joel D., and Walker, Jack L. "Political Trust and Racial Ideology." *American Political Science Review* 64 (December 1970): 1200–1202.
————. *Race in the City.* Boston: Little, Brown, 1973.
Abrahams, Roger D. *Deep Down in the Jungle.* Chicago: Aldine Publishing, 1970.
————. *Positively Black.* Englewood Cliffs, N.J.: Prentice-Hall, 1969.
Adelson, Joseph, and O'Neill, Robert. "Growth of Political Ideas in Adolescence." In *Learning About Politics,* edited by Roberta S. Sigel. New York: Random House, 1970.
Adler, Norman, and Harrington, Charles. *The Learning of Political Behavior.* Glenview, Ill.: Scott Foresman, 1970.
Agee, James. *A Death in the Family.* New York: Avon Books, 1959.
Agee, James, and Evans, Walker. *Let Us Now Praise Famous Men.* Boston: Houghton Mifflin, 1960.
Allen, Vernon L., *Psychological Factors in Poverty.* Chicago: Markham Publishing, 1970.
Allport, Gordon. *The Nature of Prejudice.* Reading, Mass.: Addison-Wesley, 1954.
Alvik, Trond. "The Development of Views on Conflict, War and Peace Among School Children." *Journal of Peace Research* 5 (1968): 171–195.
Axelrod, Robert. "The Structure of Public Opinion on Policy Issues." *Public Opinion Quarterly* 31 (Spring 1967): 49–60.

Bakan, David. *The Duality of Human Existence.* Chicago: Rand-McNally, 1966.
Baldwin, James. *Notes of a Native Son.* Boston: Beacon, 1955.
Banks, J. "Relevant Social Studies for Black Pupils." *Social Education* 33 (1969): 69–79.
Beradt, C. *The Third Reich of Dreams.* New York: Quadrangle, 1968.
Billingsley, Andrew. *Black Families in White America.* Englewood Cliffs, N.J.: Prentice-Hall, 1968.

Birnbaum, Norman. *The Crisis of Industrial Society*. New York: Oxford, 1969.
Blauner, Robert. "Internal Colonialism and Ghetto Revolt." *Social Problems* 16 (Spring 1969): 393–408.
———. *Racial Oppression in America*. New York: Harper and Row, 1972.
Blos, Peter. *On Adolescence: A Psychoanalytic Interpretation*. New York: Free Press, 1962.
Brink, William, and Harris, Louis. *The Negro Revolution in America*. New York: Simon and Schuster, 1964.
Brody, Judy. "The Child of Poverty." *Boston Globe Sunday Magazine* (April 1, 1973): 26–29.
Brown, Claude. *Manchild in the Promised Land*. New York: Macmillan, 1965.
Buxbaum, Edith. *Troubled Children in a Troubled World*. New York: International Universities Press, 1970.

Cammarota, Gloria. "Children, Politics, and Elementary Social Studies." *Social Education* (April 1963): 205–210.
Carmichael, Stokely S., and Hamilton, Charles V. *Black Power: The Politics of Liberation in America*. New York: Random House, 1968.
Clark, Donald H., and Kadis, Asya L. *Humanistic Teaching*. Columbus, O.: Charles E. Merrill Publishing, 1971.
Clark, Kenneth B. *Dark Ghetto: Dilemmas of Social Power*. New York: Harper and Row, 1965.
———. *Prejudice and Your Child*. Boston: Beacon, 1963.
Clarke, Austin. *The Meeting Point*. Boston: Little, Brown, 1967.
Cleaver, Eldridge. *Soul on Ice*. New York: McGraw-Hill, 1968.
Cohen, Dorothy H., and Stern, Virginia. *Observing and Recording the Behavior of Young Children*. New York: Teachers College Press, Columbia University, 1958.
Cohen, Jonathan. *Humanistic Psychology*. New York: Collier Books, 1962, pp. 103–124.
Coles, Robert. "Children of the American Ghetto." *Harper's Magazine* (September 1967). Volume 235, 16–22.
———. *Children of Crisis*. Boston: Atlantic–Little, Brown, 1967.
———. *Migrants, Sharecroppers, Mountaineers. Children of Crisis*, vol. 2. Boston: Atlantic–Little, Brown, 1971.
———. *The South Goes North. Children of Crisis*, vol. 3. Boston: Atlantic–Little, Brown, 1971.
———. *Still Hungry in America*. New York: World Publishing, 1969.
———. "The Words and Music of Social Change." *Daedalus* 98 (1969): 184–198.

Coles, Robert, and Piers, Maria. *The Wages of Neglect.* New York: Quadrangle, 1969.

Coopersmith, S. *The Antecedents of Self-Esteem.* San Francisco: W. H. Freeman, 1967.

Cottle, Thomas J. *The Abandoners: Portraits of Loss, Separation and Neglect.* Boston: Little, Brown, 1972.

―――. "Matilda Rutherford: She's What You Would Call a Whore." *Antioch Review* 31 (Winter, 1971–1972): 519–543.

―――. "No Way to Look but Back." *Inequality in Education* 12 (July 1972): 4–9.

―――. "A Phalanx of Children." *Appalachian Journal* 1 (Autumn 1972): 27–34.

―――. *Time's Children: Impressions of Youth.* Boston: Little, Brown, 1971.

―――. *The Voices of School: Educational Issues Through Personal Accounts.* Boston: Little, Brown, 1973.

Daniels, John. *In Freedom's Birthplace: A Study of the Boston Negroes.* New York: Negro Universities Press, Greenwood Press, Inc., 1968.

David, Jay, ed. *Growing Up Black.* New York: Morrow, 1968.

Davidson, Bruce. *The Negro American.* Boston: Houghton Mifflin, 1966.

Davis, Allison, and Dollard, John. *Children of Bondage.* New York: Harper and Row, 1960.

Dawson, Richard, and Prewitt, Kenneth. *Political Socialization.* Boston: Little, Brown, 1969.

Dennison, George. *The Lives of Children.* New York: Random House, 1969.

Deutsch, Martin. *The Disadvantaged Child.* New York: Basic Books, 1967.

―――. "The Role of Social Class in Language Development and Cognition." *American Journal of Orthopsychiatry* 35 (January 1965): 78–88.

Deutsch, Martin, and Brown, Bert. "Social Influences in Negro-White Intelligence Differences." *Journal of Social Issues* 20 (April 1964): 24–35.

Dixon, Vernon J., and Foster, Badi, eds. *Beyond Black or White.* Boston: Little, Brown, 1971.

Drake, St. Clair, and Cayton, Horace R. *Black Metropolis.* Rev. ed. New York: Harcourt Brace Jovanovich, 1970.

DuBois, W. E. B. *The Philadelphia Negro: A Social Study.* New York: Schocken, 1970.

180   BLACK CHILDREN, WHITE DREAMS

Earle, William. *The Autobiographical Consciousness: A Philosophical Inquiry into Existence.* Chicago: Quadrangle, 1972.
Easton, David, and Dennis, Jack. *Children in the Political System.* New York: McGraw-Hill, 1969.
Easton, David, and Hess, Robert. "The Child's Political World." *Midwest Journal of Political Science* 6 (August 1962): 229–246.
———. "Youth and the Political System." In *Culture and the Social Character: The Work of David Riesman Reviewed,* edited by S. M. Lipset and L. Lowenthal. New York: Free Press, 1962.
Ellison, Ralph. *The Invisible Man.* New York: Modern Library, 1963.
Erikson, Erik H. *Childhood and Society.* New York: Norton, 1950.
———. *Identity: Youth and Crisis.* New York: Norton, 1968.
———. "Identity and the Life Cycle." *Psychological Issues* 1 (1959). Whole.
———. *Insight and Responsibility.* New York: Norton, 1964.
———. *Young Man Luther.* New York: Norton, 1958.
Evans, E. Belle; Shub, Beth; and Weinstein, Marlene. *Day Care: How to Plan, Develop and Operate a Day Care Center.* Boston: Beacon, 1971.
Eysenck, H. J. *The Psychology of Politics.* New York: Praeger, 1954.

Fanon, Frantz. *Black Skin, White Masks.* Translated by Charles L. Markmann. New York: Grove Press, 1967.
———. *The Wretched of the Earth.* Translated by Constance Farrington. New York: Grove Press, 1968.
Ferdinand, T. N. "Psychological Femininity and Political Liberalism." *Sociometry* 27 (1964): 75–87.
Frazier, E. Franklin. *Black Bourgeoisie.* Glencoe, Ill.: Free Press, 1957.
———. *The Negro in the United States.* New York: Macmillan, 1957.
Freud, Anna. *Normality and Pathology in Childhood.* New York: International Universities Press, 1965.
Freud, Anna, and Burlingame, Dorothy. *War and Children.* New York: Ernst Willard, 1943.
Friedman, Murray. "Is White Racism the Problem?" *Commentary* 47 (January 1969): 61–65.

Gardner, Riley W., and Moriarty, Alice. *Personality Development at Preadolescence.* Seattle: University of Washington Press, 1968.
Garfinkle, H. *Studies in Ethnomethodology.* Englewood Cliffs, N.J.: Prentice-Hall, 1967.
Gitlin, Todd, and Hollander, Nanci. *Uptown: Poor Whites in Chicago.* New York: Harper and Row, 1970.

Glazer, Nona Y., and Creedon, Carol F., eds. *Children and Poverty: Some Sociological and Psychological Perspectives.* Chicago: Rand-McNally, 1970.

Goethals, George W., and Klos, Dennis. *Experiencing Youth.* Boston: Little, Brown, 1970.

Goffman, Erving. *The Presentation of Self in Everyday Life.* Garden City, N.Y.: Anchor Books, 1959.

Goodman, Mary E. *Race Awareness in Young Children.* New York: Collier Books, 1964.

Gordon, Chad. "Self-Conceptions Methodologies." *Journal of Nervous and Mental Disease* 148 (April 1969): 328–364.

Greenberg, Edward S. "Black Children in the Political System." *Public Opinion Quarterly* 34 (Fall 1970): 333–345.

———. "Children and Government: A Comparison Across Racial Lines." *Midwest Journal of Political Science* 14 (May 1970): 249–275.

Greene, Mary Frances, and Ryan, Orlette. *The School Children: Growing Up in the Slums.* New York: Random House, 1966.

Greenstein, Fred I. "The Benevolent Leader: Children's Images of Political Authority." *American Political Science Review* 54 (1960): 934–943.

———. *Children and Politics.* New Haven: Yale University Press, 1965.

Grier, W. H., and Cobbs, P. M. *Black Rage.* New York: Basic Books, 1968.

Grimes, A. P. *Equality in America.* New York: Oxford, 1964.

Handlin, Oscar, and Handlin, Mary F. *Facing Life: Youth and the Family in American History.* Boston: Little, Brown, 1971.

Hannerz, Ulf. *Soulside: Inquiries into Ghetto Culture and Community.* New York: Columbia University Press, 1969.

Hauser, Stuart. *Black and White Identity Formation: Explorations in the Psychological Development of White and Negro Male Adolescents.* New York: John Wiley, 1971.

Henry, Jules. *Pathways to Madness.* New York: Random House, 1971.

Herndon, James. *The Way It Spozed to Be.* New York: Simon and Schuster, 1968.

Herskovits, Melville J., and Herskovits, Frances. *The Myth of the Negro Past.* Boston: Beacon, 1958.

Hess, Robert D. "The Transmission of Cognitive Strategies in Poor Families: The Socialization of Apathy and Underachievement." In *Psychological Factors in Poverty,* edited by Vernon L. Allen. Chicago: Markham Publishing, 1970.

Hess, Robert D., and Easton, David. "The Child's Changing Image of the President." *Public Opinion Quarterly* 64 (1960): 632–644.
————. "The Role of the Elementary School in Political Socialization." *School Review* (Autumn 1962): 252–265.
Hess, Robert D., and Torney, Judith. *The Development of Political Attitudes in Children.* Chicago: Aldine Publishing, 1967.
Hill, B., and Burke, N. "Some Disadvantaged Youths Look at Their Schools." *Journal of Negro Education* 37 (1968): 135–139.
Horowitz, Eugene L. "Some Aspects of the Development of Patriotism in Children." *Sociometry* 3 (1940): 329–341.
Hughes, Langston. *Montage of a Dream Deferred.* New York: Holt, 1951.
Hughes, Langston, and Bontemps, Arna. *The Book of Negro Folklore.* New York: Dodd, Mead, 1958.
Hunt, J. McV. *Intelligence and Experience.* New York: Ronald Press, 1961.
Hyman, Herbert. *Political Socialization.* Glencoe, Ill.: Free Press, 1959.

Jaros, Dean. "Children's Orientation Toward the President: Some Additional Theoretical Considerations and Data." *Journal of Politics* 29 (May 1969): 368–387.
Jennings, M. Kent. "Patterns of Political Learning." *Harvard Educational Review* 30 (Summer 1968): 443–467.
Jennings, M. Kent, and Niemi, Richard. "The Transmission of Political Values from Parent to Child." *American Political Science Review* 62 (1968): 169–184.
Jones, Leroi. *Two Plays: The Dutchman and The Slave.* New York: Apollo, 1966.

Kagan, Jerome. *Understanding Children: Behavior, Motives and Thought.* New York: Harcourt Brace Jovanovich, 1971.
Kagan, Jerome, and Coles, Robert, eds. *Twelve to Sixteen: Early Adolescence.* New York: Norton, 1972.
Kagan, Jerome, and Moss, Howard. *Birth to Maturity: Study in Psychological Development.* New York: John Wiley, 1962.
Kardiner, Abram, and Ovesey, Lionel. *The Mark of Oppression.* New York: Norton, 1951.
Keil, Charles. *Urban Blues.* Chicago: University of Chicago Press, 1966.
Keniston, Kenneth. "Youth: A 'New' Stage of Life." *American Scholar* 39 (1970): 631–654.

Kolaja, Jiri. *Social System and Time and Space*. Pittsburgh: Duquesne University Press, 1961
Kovel, Joel. *White Racism: A Psychohistory*. New York: Pantheon, 1970.
Kozol, Jonathan. *Death at an Early Age*. Boston: Houghton Mifflin, 1967.

Laing, R. D. *The Politics of Experience*. New York: Pantheon, 1967.
Lane, Robert E. *Political Life*. Glencoe, Ill.: Free Press, 1959.
Langer, Thomas S; Herson, Joseph H; Greene, Edward L.; Jameson, Jean D.; and Goff, Jeanne A. "Children of the City: Affluence, Poverty and Mental Health." In *Psychological Factors in Poverty*, edited by Vernon L. Allen. Chicago: Markham Publishing, 1970.
Lasswell, Harold. *Power and Personality*. New York: Viking, 1963.
Lawson, Edwin D. "Development of Patriotism in Children: A Second Look." In *The Learning of Political Behavior*, edited by Norman Adler and Charles Harrington. Glenview, Ill.: Scott Foresman, 1970.
Lewis, M. M. *Language, Thought and Personality in Infancy and Childhood*. New York: Basic Books, 1963.
Lewis, Oscar. *Children of Sanchez*. New York: Random House, 1961.
————. *Five Families: Mexican Case Studies in the Culture of Poverty*. New York: Basic Books, 1959.
————. *La Vida*. New York: Random House, 1965.
Liebow, Elliot. *Tally's Corner: A Study of Negro Streetcorner Men*. Boston: Little, Brown, 1967.
Lightfoot, Sara Lawrence. "An Ethnographic Study of the Status Structure of the Classroom." Unpublished Dissertation, Harvard University, Graduate School of Education, 1972.
Litwack, Leo. *North of Slavery*. Chicago: University of Chicago Press, 1961.
Loewald, Hans W. "Ego and Reality." *International Journal of Psychoanalysis* 32 (1951): 10–18.
Lomax, Louis E. *The Negro Revolt*. New York: Harper and Row, 1962.
Looft, William R. *Developmental Psychology: A Book of Readings*. Hinsdale, Ill.: Dryden Press, 1972.
Lyons, Schley R. "The Political Socialization of Ghetto Children: Efficacy and Cynicism." *Journal of Politics* 32 (May 1970): 288–304.

Maccoby, Eleanor E.; Matthews, Richard E.; and Morton, Anton S. "Youth and Political Change." *Public Opinion Quarterly* (Spring 1954): 23–39.

McClelland, David C. *The Roots of Consciousness.* Princeton: Van Nostrand Reinhold, 1964.

Malcolm X. *The Autobiography of Malcolm X.* New York: Grove Press, 1965.

Marshall, Kim. *Law and Order in Grade 6–E.* Boston: Little, Brown, 1972.

Marx, Gary T. *Protest and Prejudice.* New York: Harper and Row, 1967.

May, Rollo. *The Meaning of Anxiety.* New York: Ronald Press, 1950.

May, Rollo; Angel, Ernest; and Ellenberger, Henri F., eds. *Existence.* New York: Basic Books, 1958.

Meier, A., and Rudiwick, E. M. *From Plantation to Ghetto.* New York: Hill and Wang, 1966.

Miller, Daniel R., and Swanson, Guy E. *Inner Conflict and Defense.* New York: Holt, 1960.

Mitscherlich, Alexander. *Society Without the Father.* New York: Harcourt, Brace and World, 1969.

Morland, K. J. "Racial Recognition by Nursery School Children in Lynchburg, Virginia." *Social Forces* 37 (1958): 132–137.

O'Gorman, Ned. *The Wilderness and the Laurel Tree.* New York: Harper and Row, 1972.

Olsen, Marvin E. "Social and Political Participation of Blacks." *American Sociological Review* 35 (August 1970): 682–697.

Orum, Anthony M., ed. *The Seeds of Politics: Youth and Politics in America.* Englewood Cliffs, N.J.: Prentice-Hall, 1972.

Orum, Anthony M., and Cohen, Roberta S. "The Development of Political Orientations Among Black and White Children." *American Sociological Review* 38 (February 1973): 62–74.

Parsons, Talcott. "Youth in the Context of American Society." *Daedalus* 91 (Winter 1962): 97–123.

Parsons, Talcott, and Clark, Kenneth B., eds. *The Negro American.* Boston: Houghton Mifflin, 1966.

Pettigrew, Thomas F. *A Profile of the Negro American.* Princeton: Van Nostrand Reinhold, 1964.

——. *Racially Separate or Together?* New York: McGraw Hill, 1971.

Porter, Judith. *Black Child, White Child: The Development of Racial Attitudes.* Cambridge: Harvard University Press, 1971.

Poussaint, Alvin F. "Education and Black Self Concept." *Freedomways* 18 (1968): 334–339.

Rainwater, Lee. *Behind Ghetto Walls*. Chicago: Aldine Publishing, 1970.

Raph, Jane Beasely. "Language Development in Socially Disadvantaged Children." *Review of Educational Research* 35 (December 1965): 389–397.

Redl, Fritz. *When We Deal with Children*. New York: Free Press, 1966.

Riessman, Frank. *The Culturally Deprived Child*. New York: Harper and Row, 1962.

Riis, Jacob A. *How the Other Half Lives*. New York: Dover, 1970.

Ritchie, Oscar W., and Kokler, Marvin R. *Sociology of Childhood*. New York: Appleton-Century Crofts, 1964.

Rokeach, Milton. *The Open and Closed Mind*. New York: Basic Books, 1960.

———. "Political and Religious Dogmatism: An Alternative to the Authoritarian Personality." *Psychological Monographs* 70 (1956): (18, whole number 425).

Roszak, Theodore. *The Making of a Counter-Culture: Reflections on the Technocratic Society and Its Youthful Opposition*. Garden City, N.Y.: Doubleday, 1969.

Rubin, Lillian B. *Busing and Backlash: White Against White in an Urban School District*. Berkeley: University of California Press, 1972.

Rudofsky, Bernard. *Streets for People: A Primer for Americans*. Garden City, N.Y.: Doubleday, 1969.

Sarbin, Theodore R. "Role Theory." In *Handbook of Social Psychology*, vol. 1, edited by Gardner Lindzey, Reading, Mass.: Addison-Wesley, 1954.

Schuman, Howard, and Greenberg, Barry. "The Impact of City on Racial Attitudes." *American Journal of Sociology* 76 (September 1970): 213–262.

Schwartz, B. "The Social Psychology of Privacy." *American Journal of Sociology* 73 (May 1968): 741–752.

Sheatsley, Paul B. "White Attitudes Toward the Negro." *Daedalus* 95 (Winter 1966): 217–238.

Sigel, I. E. "How Intelligence Tests Limit Understanding of Intelligence." *Merrill-Palmer Quarterly of Behavior and Development* 9: 39–56.

Sigel, Roberta S., ed. *Learning About Politics*. New York: Random House, 1970.

Sigel, Roberta S. An Exploration into Some Aspects of Socialization:

School Children's Reactions to the Death of a President." In *Children and the Death of a President*, edited by Martha Wolfenstein and Gilbert Kliman. Garden City, N.Y.: Doubleday, 1965.

Simpson, G. E., and Yinger, J. M. *Racial and Cultural Minorities*. 3d ed. New York: Harper and Row, 1965.

Skolnick, Jerome H. *The Politics of Protest*. New York: Simon and Schuster, 1969.

Slater, Philip E. *The Pursuit of Loneliness: American Culture at the Breaking Point*. Boston: Beacon, 1970.

Smith, Lillian. *Killers of the Dream*. Garden City, N.Y.: Anchor Books, 1963.

Smith, M. Brewster. "Competence and Socialization." In *Socialization and Society*, edited by J. A. Clausen. Boston: Little, Brown, 1968.

Spiegelberg, H. *The Phenomenological Movement*. Vols. 1 and 2. The Hague: Martinus Nijhoff, 1965.

Stein, Herman D., ed. *Planning for the Needs of Children in Developing Nations*. New York: United Nations Children's Fund, 1964.

Stock, Irvin. "Black Literature, Relevance and the New Irrationality." *Change Magazine* 3 (March/April 1971): 43–49.

Stoddard, G. D. *The Meaning of Intelligence*. New York: Macmillan, 1943.

Strouse, Jean. *Up Against the Law: The Legal Rights of People Under 21*. New York: New American Library, 1970.

Taeuber, Karl E., and Taeuber, Alma F. *Negroes in Cities*. Chicago: Aldine Publishing, 1964.

Targ, Harry. "Children's Developing Orientations to International Politics." *Journal of Peace Research* 7 (1970): 80–98.

Thomas, Piri. *Down These Mean Streets*. New York: Knopf, 1967.

Tolley, Howard, Jr. *Children and War*. New York: Teachers College Press, Columbia University, 1973.

Uslander, Arlene; Weiss, Caroline; Telman, Judith; Wernick, Esona; in collaboration with Higgins, James V. *Their Universe*. New York: Delacorte, 1973.

Vontress, C. E. "The Negro Personality Reconsidered." *Journal of Negro Education* 35 (1966): 210–222.

Wallach, Michael A., and Wing, Jr., Cliff W. *The Talented Student: A Validation of the Creativity-Intelligence Distinction*. New York: Holt, 1969.

Walters, James; Connor, Ruth; and Zunich, Michael. "Interaction of Mothers and Children from Lower Class Families." *Child Development* 35 (June 1964): 433–440.

Warren, Robert Penn. *Who Speaks for the Negro?* New York: Random House, 1965.

Weinstein, Fred, and Platt, Gerald M. *Psychoanalytic Sociology.* Baltimore: Johns Hopkins Press, 1973.

———. *The Wish to Be Free.* Berkeley: University of California Press, 1969.

Wheelis, Allen. *The Quest for Identity.* New York: Norton, 1958.

White, Robert W. "Motivation Reconsidered: The Concept of Competence." *Psychological Review* 66 (1959): 297–333.

Whiting, John W., and Child, Irving R. *Child Training and Personality.* New Haven: Yale University Press, 1953.

Whyte, William Foote. *Street Corner Society.* Chicago: University of Chicago Press, 1955.

Williams, John A. *The Man Who Cried I Am.* Boston: Little, Brown, 1967.

Wilson, Alan B. "Residential Segregation of Social Class and Aspirations of High School Boys." *American Sociological Review* 24 (December 1959): 836–845.

Wolfenstein, Martha. *Children's Humor.* Glencoe, Ill.: Free Press, 1954.

Wolfenstein, Martha, and Kliman, Gilbert, eds. *Children and the Death of a President.* Garden City, N.Y.: Doubleday, 1965.

Wright, Richard. *Native Son.* New York: Harper and Row, 1940.

Ziajka, Alan. "The Black Youth's Self Concept." In *Developmental Psychology: A Book of Readings,* edited by William P. Looft. Hinsdale, Ill.: Dryden Press, 1972.